# The Second Rape

# The Second Rape

*Society's Continued Betrayal
of the Victim*

Lee Madigan, Ph.D.
Nancy C. Gamble, Ph.D.

LEXINGTON BOOKS
*An Imprint of Macmillan, Inc.*
NEW YORK

Maxwell Macmillan Canada
TORONTO

Maxwell Macmillan International
NEW YORK   OXFORD   SINGAPORE   SYDNEY

Grateful acknowledgment is made
for permission to reprint selections from
*Refusing to Be a Man*.
Copyright © 1989 by John Stoltenberg.
Reproduced by permission of John Stoltenberg.

Library of Congress Cataloging-in-Publication Data

Madigan, Lee.
The second rape: society's continued betrayal of the victim / Lee Madigan,
Nancy C. Gamble.
p. cm.
ISBN 0-669-27189-6
1. Rape—United States—Psychological aspects. 2. Rape victims—
United States—Psychology. 3. Rape victims—Services for—United
States—Psychological aspects. I. Gamble, Nancy C. II. Title.
HV6561.G35   1991
362.88'3—dc20                                                                    91-8257
                                                                                        CIP

Lexington Books
An Imprint of Macmillan, Inc.
866 Third Avenue, New York, N. Y. 10022

Maxwell Macmillan Canada, Inc.
1200 Eglinton Avenue East
Suite 200
Don Mills, Ontario M3C 3N1

Macmillan, Inc. is part of the Maxwell Communication
Group of Companies.

Printed in the United States of America

printing number
1 2 3 4 5 6 7 8 9 10

*This book is dedicated to*
*the courageous men and women everywhere*
*who speak of their crimes.*

# Contents

**PART THREE**

# The Second Rapists

**PART FOUR**

# Empowerment

# Preface

In 1958, the term *sexual* was whispered. Sexual assault was not even acknowledged. A fearful eighth-grader in a large high school stood at her locker one day when a black male seemed to come out of nowhere. He put his hand up her skirt and felt between her legs and buttocks. She later learned that the slang term for this act was *goosing*. He undoubtedly saw the look of shock on her face. She told no one. She might never have told anyone, but he kept stalking her for days. The same act occurred eight to ten times more. Each time it seemed as if he appeared from nowhere, and each time he wore a sadistic smile. The look on his face was imprinted on her mind forever. Her heart would beat in her throat the moment she got on the bus to go to school.

The young girl wondered why he was doing this to her. The shame was immense. She thought that maybe her skirt was too tight or provocative, so she started wearing full skirts. This only made it easier for him to attack. The only reason she was brave enough to tell was that her fear mounted to the point where she was afraid he would follow her home and rape her. She told her mother, who kept very quiet. After all, those kinds of things didn't happen to middle-class families in Kansas.

Finally she told the principal of the high school. He said that the boy had been suspended because of similar complaints from others over the past year. So it wasn't just her! For months after his suspension, the young girl was hypervigilant and frightened of all black males. Because of the principal's casual attitude, she was sure his suspension would be short, so she lived in fear until she finally requested a transfer out of that school. She had to leave her friends and all that was familiar to her, but her fear was immense. Suspension was only a slap on the hand, for the boy's behavior may well have escalated to rape. This girl was not actually raped, but she experienced the second rape—apathy from those she told and the need to flee for her own sense of safety.

The late 1960s brought social unrest and with it gang violence. A young woman was driving to the Laundromat at dusk on what was a main thoroughfare through town. This particular evening, the street was eerily void of all cars. She came upon a car on fire blocking the road, and a group of fifteen to twenty high-school-age boys and girls descended on her car and beckoned her to help. Trusting their intentions, she opened the car door. Instead, they took her purse and dragged her out into the street. They proceeded to rip off her clothes and hit her over the head with a brick. They said they were going to rape and kill her.

The young woman watched this violent frenzy as if from a distance. This couldn't be happening. Surely she would awaken from the nightmare soon. If not, she prayed that she would faint. As they were arguing over their plan, she saw a tow truck coming toward her. She broke from the group and ran in front of the truck to get it to stop. The driver almost didn't take her in, but she managed to fling herself into the cab, bloody and unclothed.

The worst was yet to come. She told the police officer at the emergency room that she could identify some of her assaulters. He just nodded. Later her telephone calls to the police were never returned. She looked for some mention of the attack in the newspaper, but there was none. After all, it was explained, to acknowledge gang violence would hurt the city's tourism economy. Her husband said, "Just be glad you're alive and okay. We don't want them coming after you."

Disillusionment set in. Where was the posse that was supposed to rescue the damsel in distress? Several weeks later, she started to relate the story to another couple over martinis. She felt a kick under the table, and her husband said, "Not at dinner, dear." So this incident in which she had almost lost her life was pushed far into the back of her mind. This young woman had survived a second rape.

We know what it feels like to be the target of sexually aggressive acts. We lived through the above experiences. We also know firsthand that reporting these acts can lead to even greater feelings of violation and trauma. It is ironic, however, that we made our identifications as survivors rather belatedly—well into the writing of this book. This attests to the great lengths to which women will go to make sure that rape or sexual violation is "not me." It underscores the depth of repression that is necessary to carry on with the sometimes frightening experience of being female in our society.

Despite our years of experience and the book knowledge we had in the area of sexual assault, we were ignorant about some aspects of it. It wasn't until we had walked in a survivor's shoes by attending rape trials, interviewing police, and networking with prosecuting attorneys that we could truly empathize. Unfortunately, many therapists working with survivors may be poorly trained to understand the rape that society perpetrates after a woman reports. Therapists can be second rapists, too, if they are ignorant and unwilling to accept the woman's reality once she tells. We have all been so brainwashed by certain ideas about men, women, and rape that even the most educated and sophisticated among us do harm. We can no longer sit in our ivory towers pretending that all is right with the world but wrong with our clients.

We are writing this book with the hope that *all* people can benefit from our investigation. It is unfortunate that it takes living through a rape or having a loved one raped to understand what it's all about.

# Acknowledgments

**W**e are indebted to all the people who sacrificed hours of their valuable time to be interviewed by us. We appreciated the candor and interest of many attorneys, doctors, and police officers. This book was made possible by their knowledge and generous contributions. Special thanks to Laurie McKenzie and Jean Wright and her coworkers, who were particularly helpful in sharing their insights and leading us to resources that could deepen our understanding. To our assistant editor, Lyri Merrill, we are forever indebted for the names of wonderful books without which our history of rape would have been incomplete.

Over a period of ten years, we have listened to and felt with hundreds of rape survivors. It is impossible to do the work we do without feeling touched by these women's pain and awed by their courage. In retrospect, we feel honored that they trusted us. We are especially thankful for the four survivors who gave us countless hours of their time and emotional energy so that we could record their personal stories of violation. We are sure that their experience with us was sometimes excruciating and tedious. We thank these women and hope that their efforts in sharing help others.

Lastly, we want to thank the women in the survivors support group who in early 1989 brought to our attention the injustices that they had experienced after they reported. They were the real catalysts for the investigation that led to this book. Thank goodness we listened.

# PART ONE

# Introduction

# 1

# After the Crime

This is a story that needs to be told. It's not a pretty story. *Rape* itself is an ugly word, but this book carries the meaning of the word *rape* even further. There is a new, more disturbing twist to rape if one becomes aware that women who report a rape are again raped by a system composed of well-intentioned people who are nevertheless blinded by the myths of centuries.

It's impossible not to know that a second rape is occurring. The statistics speak for themselves. Based on reports to the police, sixteen rapes are attempted and ten women are raped every hour (U.S. House 1990). That's *reported*. How many occur and go unreported? According to Susan Estrich (1987), rape is the single most underreported major crime. Experts estimate that only 10 percent of sexual assaults are brought to the police (U.S. House 1990). Interpolating the above data, this means that sexual assault is occurring to 100 women an hour, or once every 36 seconds. Sexual assault is attempted on 160 women an hour, or once every 22.5 seconds. There must be some very serious rationale to explain this underreporting and why we as a society have tolerated these horrific statistics.

We can begin by stating that our society vehemently denies the frequent occurrence of rape. In fact, as you are reading this page, a woman somewhere has suddenly found herself in an unpredictable and dangerous situation. She will be forced to submit to the most private and intimate acts against her will. Making love has become twisted. It is no longer a sacred sharing but hate and power expressed by violence and brutality. The violation may occur with a weapon present, or she may simply be caught off guard by someone she trusts. She may resist and struggle or remain passive in order to save her life. Regardless, the shock and inability to reason with her attacker make her situation terrifying.

It is obviously easier for women to deny that a sexual violation is rape, and so crime statistics don't reflect its true frequency. If the question "Have you ever been forced to have sex?" is posed rather than the question "Have you ever been raped?" a very serious picture emerges. An estimated 15 to 40 percent of women are victims of attempted or completed rapes during their lifetimes (U.S. House 1990). Three separate studies of college students released in 1985 indicated that one in five women in each study disclosed being "physically forced to have intercourse by her date" (Estrich 1987).

Many people also believe that rape can occur only to "women who live the wrong way": those that are sexually loose, foolhardy, uneducated, lower class, and above all mentally unstable. From our experience, rape survivors can be checkers at the local supermarket, attorneys, teachers, or even police investigators. They can be sisters, mothers, daughters, or next-door neighbors. Most importantly, if you are female, the victim could be you.

It is also commonly thought that rape can occur only in dangerous surroundings and be committed only by a stranger with a weapon. However, 50 to 70 percent of all rapes occur in the context of an ongoing relationship with varying degrees of trust existing (U.S. House 1990). In a survey of 3,187 college women, 478 reported having been raped. Of those raped, 10.6 percent were raped by strangers, 24.9 percent by nonromantic acquaintances, 21 percent by casual dates, 30 percent by steady dates, and 8.9 percent by family members (U.S. House 1990). A rapist can be a boyfriend, husband's friend, or colleague at work.

Many people assume that rapists have psychopathic personalities and are detectable at first glance. This is an erroneous notion. Rapists do have something in common, though. They use sex as a weapon. Rape is an aggressive act that gives the offender a sense of power and allows him to discharge anger. The act can be accompanied by brutal violence or verbal intimidation, but the motive is always dominance and control. Rapists are not usually people already identified as criminals, though it is typical for them to rape many times again if not apprehended (U.S. House 1990).

Perhaps you've heard these facts before. Rape is not a rare occurrence. It often happens to someone or is committed by someone we know. For some reason, however, the impact eludes us. The problem is that we say we believe the preceding statements, but at our very core, we do not. This book bears this out.

Before going any further, it is necessary to acknowledge some progress in the area of the "first rape"—the actual crime society has finally recognized as reportable to the police and prosecutable by the state. We and many others would like to think that progress has been made in the past decade toward instating a victim's rights. She may now be entitled to advocacy and financial restitution from the perpetrator. In many states, more services are available, especially in the form of crisis intervention and hot lines.

Particularly in the mental health professions, society also has gained an understanding of the emotional suffering a survivor endures because of the first rape. The mental health profession is familiar with the symptoms of posttraumatic stress disorder, which is the psychiatric diagnosis most commonly applied to rape victims. Posttraumatic stress disorder as a syndrome manifests itself most often by the victim's reexperiencing a traumatic event.

A rape survivor often fears her dreams because she relives the attack. She sees again the look of hatred in her attacker's face, smells his odor, hears his degradation. She is frozen in fear and awakes, drenched in a cold sweat, gasping for air. Sleep, with its vulnerability and loss of control, becomes something to be dreaded and feared. Recurrent daytime flashbacks also are common.

The victim may run in fear from any man on the street who resembles her attacker. She may search desperately for a rest room in which she can regurgitate. An unexpected touch on her shoulder prompts a startle reflex, and the woman braces for an assault and possibly death. The rape survivor cannot escape from her own mind, which is now, as in the event itself, under the control of the rapist. Once pleasurable activities are forgotten as though they existed in another lifetime. She withdraws from herself and is alone in a cell with no walls. She is held prisoner by someone unseen for months, maybe years. The terror may never leave. Certainly, she will never be the same.

The "second rape" is the act of violation, alienation, and disparagement a survivor receives when she turns to others for help and support. It can occur only if she has been brave enough to tell someone of her assault. Keeping the rape a secret will prevent the second rape from occurring. Nevertheless, many survivors assume that friends and loved ones will be supportive. Instead, a possessive husband may become outraged by the spoiling of his property. He may condemn her for what she was wearing or where she went on the day of the assault. According to our sample of two hundred rape survivors, one-half to two-thirds of all intimate male-female relationships are severed by revelation of rape. Friends may withdraw from her due to their own discomfort, about not knowing what to say. They also may be reminded of their own vulnerability and therefore wish to believe that the rape never happened.

Lack of support also occurs with professional people who have contact with the survivor. Some physicians who treat the postrape survivor are insensitive to her. Even female physicians have been known to say, "How did you get yourself in this fix, honey?" One example of this nonsupport was Laura's experience following a rape by her landlord. Laura was devoutly religious. Several months following her assault, no amount of reassurance could penetrate the deepening guilt she felt for having been raped. Finally, she approached the pastor of her church and asked for forgiveness. Instead he replied, "You were raped by this man because you haven't been walking with God. You had already committed a sin by sleeping with your fiancé. You deserved your ill fate."

Fortunately, Laura and others have been able to shake off the hostility and condemnation of others. Unfortunately, it is these people who are in the best position to influence the survivor's well-being. Women like Laura have gone on to make much-needed changes in their lives. This is testimony to these women's will to endure despite the unfavorable odds.

The feelings of despondency and self-doubt that deepen in the survivor because of the treatment of those around her are not imagined. A woman's rage at her husband's lack of empathy is not displaced anger at the rapist. Her fear that she is not being taken seriously regarding the account of the rape is often accurate. Her perception that she is still in danger and will not be protected is not just a hysterical reaction to her assault. All of these feelings are very real but are not the result of the criminal act itself, the first rape. Instead, these feelings are the result of the second rape.

The second rape is exemplified most dramatically when the survivor is strong enough, brave enough, and even naive enough to believe that if she decides to prosecute her offender, justice will be done. It is a rape more devastating and despoiling than the first. This is the focus of our book. Statistics bear out the terror of the second rape. As already learned, only one out of ten rapes is reported to the police. Of those reported, approximately 20 percent of the perpetrators are convicted of rape. In 1986, for instance, 91,460 rapes were reported to the police, but only 19,685 individuals were convicted of rape (U.S. House 1990). Only two out of one hundred rapists are ever punished for the crime they have committed. Ninety-eight percent of all rapists go free.

Little has been written to explain the survivor's journey down the road toward justice. From her perspective, it is a road filled with treacherous potholes, dangerous and unexpected detours, and frustrating roadblocks. With each successive meeting with the police and the district attorney, her self-esteem decreases, and she has a desire to return from whence she came.

The symptoms we see and hear from survivors in reaction to the second rape are hysteria, rage, disillusionment, and profound distrust of people and the world in general. These feelings are in direct conflict with what the survivor has been taught to believe. Because she is unprepared for and unenlightened about the second rape, she feels that she must be crazy. She believes she has been lied to, ignored, and treated inhumanely by others. Those around her couldn't be wrong, so she begins to hate and distrust herself, setting in motion the vicious cycle of further victimization, depression, and masochism.

This book was written to expose the second rape. The most immediate purpose is to send this message to every survivor: "You're not crazy. You *are* being traumatized. Society is not your friend when it comes to rape." This message goes to the family, friends, and employers of survivors as well.

We must look to the beginning of humankind's history thirty thousand years ago to understand the underlying ideology and mythology of rape. We are indebted to the scholars who helped provide us with a comprehensive and well-documented understanding of rape as a political institution. Researchers and writers such as Susan Brownmiller, Riane Eisler, Monica Sjöö, Barbara Mor, and John

Stoltenberg helped us gain a better overall picture through their insights. The truth needs to be repeated over and over until it is heard and changes are made.

We also listened to the stories of four rape survivors. Lydia recounted her experience with classic stranger rape; Debbie told us about rape within the context of an ongoing relationship; Mercedes, a teenager, recalled her attempted rape; and Katie shared a rape that occurred while she was in the military. Although the first rapes are different, the second rapes are similar. These stories provide detailed accounts from the date of the crime through the aftermath of justice. Reliving these events was very painful for these women, and we tell their stories in their own words as much as possible. The survivors' names and any identifying information have been changed in an attempt to encourage these women to speak frankly. Most women are unable to speak easily of their torment because propriety, modesty, and acute shame inhibit a detailed retelling.

The real accounts of rape are followed by a parable of rape. This is a famous story that has been told and retold to children for centuries. Its presence in our book reflects its power in influencing our attitudes about rape and the role expectations of men and women. Note the similarities between the parable and the actual rape stories. This parable had its beginning in Paris in 1697 and still accurately reflects many public attitudes. These early childhood messages are cemented in the roots of our judgments today.

We excluded many rape stories from our small sampling because we wanted to focus on survivors' experiences in the justice system. For instance, the myriad examples we know of date or acquaintance rape are conspicuously missing. Our exclusion is not meant to infer that these women's stories are not important. They most definitely are. In fact, we could have filled an entire book from our caseload with what is, according to statistics, a rather common experience for women. However, our best guess is that few of these cases ever reach the courtroom, and the majority are dismissed even if reported (Estrich 1987). We are reminded of the young Japanese American woman who in the course of therapy casually mentioned that the previous night a friend of her boyfriend's had physically forced her to have intercourse. When her therapist, one of the authors, stated that she had been raped, the woman appeared stunned but refused to report the incident to the police because she felt responsible. We also are reminded of a twenty-three-year-old woman who was hospitalized by one of the authors because of a rape eight years earlier by her best male friend and the boyfriend of her best girlfriend. These are the rapes that are never reported. These are the rapes that are never even identified as rape. Because of our book's focus on survivors' experiences in the system, their stories are not told here.

Also, we didn't include adult male rape survivors. It is estimated that one out of twelve rape victims is a male (U.S. House 1990). Probably the acute shame they feel—more, even, than women—precludes their reporting and thus their appearance in our experience.

Finally, despite the fact that we omitted disabled persons and some ethnic groups, we tried to represent women of varying ages, education, and socioeconomic backgrounds in our survivor stories and in vignettes interspersed throughout the book.

The second part of the book consists of interviews with the second rapists, including medical and mental health personnel, police investigators, attorneys, and judges. These people have the closest professional contact with survivors after they decide to report their rape. We wanted to expose the attitudes of helpers toward those to whom they are providing a service. Our sample was small and geographically limited, but we believe that the attitudes of the professionals reported in this book are representative of those throughout the nation. We chose our interviewees based on personal regard for their work and respect for them as individuals.

These professionals became for us the epitome of society as it is today, with a tremendous capacity to do harm and not even know it. Every effort was made to protect the anonymity of our interviewees. Because of this protection, people were surprisingly candid. Some admitted openly to biased and outdated attitudes in the system in which they work. Many hoped that our book could help educate their coworkers, which is encouraging.

We gained an understanding of man's inhumanity to man, man's inhumanity to woman, and even woman's inhumanity to woman. The more people we interviewed, the angrier and more disillusioned we got. We realized that the key to change for the rape survivor cannot be found in society at the present time. Society needs to validate the experience of the second rape to improve the rate of reporting and prosecuting. Until the second rape is stopped, little will be gained by changing any written laws pertaining to the first rape.

This book is not just about rape but about the male and female behavioral expectations that provide the basis for rape. Almost everybody in his or her own way provides nourishment that allows rape to flourish and grow. Rape rates rose four times as fast as the total crime rate in the 1980s (U.S. House 1990). Each of us must search our heart and mind now so that prejudice and bias can be eliminated. Nobody escapes blame for something so extraordinarily wrong.

# 2

# Back to Basics

**R**ape may be a rather recent phenomenon in the history of *Homo sapiens*. Men and women lived on the earth some 300,000 years before the advent of patriarchy and its institutions, which repressed, controlled, and exploited female sexuality (Sjöö and Mor 1987). Western male historians have always insisted that *real* history began only 5,000 years ago. They have dismissed or suppressed our earlier heritage as primitive and spiritually undeveloped, as crude and carnal, as unworthy of study. Ancient millennia were buried, forgotten, or passed off as mythology. This has been the version of history taught in schools. Recent discoveries lead us to an alternate view, however. These discoveries cast a very different light on why rape exists and how it can be eradicated.

Historian William Irwin Thompson has this to say of our hidden ancient history: "The very language we use to discuss the past speaks of tools, hunters and men, whereas every statue and painting we discover cries out to us that Ice Age humanity was a culture of art, love of animals and women" (Sjöö and Mor 1987, 79). This evidence would indicate that the first thirty thousand years of human culture was dominated by a celebration of women. The female biological processes were revered and worshiped by both sexes. The mysteries of menstruation, pregnancy, and childbirth; the abundance of the earth; the seasonal movement of animals; and the cycles of time were the foundation of society. From the Upper Paleolithic to the Mid-Neolithic eras, the first god images painted or carved were those of females.

*women revered*

Historians and archaeologists tell us now that human culture began in Africa among black women. This society was neither primitive nor undeveloped but was the cradle of creativity. This culturally advanced civilization, which spread onto other continents, was *matrifocal*, which means "primacy of the mother." Women lived communally as men were off hunting. The identity and inheritance of children were passed along female bloodlines. Although revering the role of the mother, this was an egalitarian society, for it was not built on dominance. Men and women worked alongside each other in complementary, cooperative relationships, with neither having power or ownership over the other.

In the language of the primitives, the word *mother* means "producer," and evidence indicates that women were responsible for significant contributions to evolution. The most primal tools unearthed by archaeologists are women's digging sticks. For contemporary and historic hunting-gathering peoples, 75 to 80 percent of a group's subsistence came from the women's food-gathering activities. Women were the first to use and domesticate fire, and they were the first potters, weavers, and dyers. Women were the first doctors with knowledge of herbs to cure ailments. They were instrumental in originating language, the first scripts and glyphs; domesticating grain and animals; creating religious imagery and rituals; making laws; developing calendars; and studying astronomy. Anthropologist Evelyn Reed has stated that human culture developed out of women's labor groups, interrelations, and crafts (Sjöö and Mor 1987, 33).

Discoveries tell us that ancient women were quite different from today's women. For instance, menstruation was valued and female sexuality accepted. Ancient women had strong genital pride and knowledge and in no way envied, feared, or imitated men. Women were the initiators of sexual knowledge. Shame about one's body or one's sexuality was probably unheard of. Women made decisions about their own bodies, including when and with whom to engage in sexual relations and if and when to have children. They had a great effect on the survival and well-being of their people. And they had the communal support of other women on which to draw.

Historically, evidence reveals that the farther back we go in human history, the gentler our species was, and that matrifocal society concentrated on maintaining life rather than exploiting it. Neolithic people saw nature (trees, rocks, water, animals, and so on) as sacred. All was part of a cosmic whole through which a continuous life energy flowed. Body, mind, and spirit were integrated. It is interesting to note through the artifacts of great civilizations such as Çatal Hüyük and Crete that the great mother was androgynous, suggesting a potential unity of the sexes in mutual love and service. With the entry of patriarchy, this ontology, with its affirmation of life and lack of destructiveness, was severely threatened. The goddess culture has eventually diminished to only a trace in our genes and unconscious dreams and memories.

At some time and for reasons shrouded in mystery and lost in the prehistory of the written word, the social structure of the world changed. Militant new male gods appeared during the Late Neolithic Era or Bronze Age (c. 2800 B.C.), coinciding, some say, with the development of heavy metals and warfare (Eisler 1987). According to historical novelist Robert Graves, the major theme of the Greek myths was the gradual reduction of women from sacred beings to slaves. Women became the spoils brought home from conquered lands, and imperialism flourished (Sjöö and Mor 1987). Bronze Age males began to take over women's ancient inventions and industries to improve them by capitalizing them. Simultaneously, they took over the most primal production of all—women's production of children. Other lands, as well as cattle, women, and children, became part of men's wealth—their property. Thus did society change from kinship/tribal to urban/centralized rule, from sacred to secular, from organic to mechanical. With the division of life into higher and lower categories, the original holism and equality of matrifocal society was destroyed.

With patriarchy also came dualistic thinking. The mother goddess, once a symbol of unity, was dichotomized into extremes. Women were either idealized as the good, passive ovulating wife, rather asexual except to bear her husband's children, or the wanton sex fiend. Beginning with Eve's disobedience of a male god and the temptation of Adam in the Book of Genesis (some have mistakenly called this the beginning of history), sexual women became evil and not to be trusted. Many believed that men became jealous over women's sexual capacity and their ability to create life (Sjöö and

Mor (1987). Therefore, natural female functions were made filthy and sinful. Menstrual periods and childbirth were defined as unclean and dangerous.

For several thousand years, the goddess culture survived underground alongside patriarchy and was known as witchcraft. People who still believed in the psychic powers of women and in their ability to alleviate suffering and cure illness were suspected to be agents of the devil. The three hundred years of witch-hunts in Europe were aimed at eradicating ancient women's cultures. In Europe between 1400 and 1700, one million to nine million people (80 percent of them women) were burned as witches. Witch burners equated the devil with sexual activity. Women were raped and sexually abused by their torturers, who rationalized these acts as an exorcism of the devil.

Patriarchal systems became obsessed with keeping their female property chaste. It would seem that women needed to be restrained by men or male institutions so as not to wreak havoc with "civilization." The Romans invented the technique of fastening metal clasps through the prepuces of young girls to enforce chastity (infibulation). Presumably to maintain the good honor of his wife, a knight riding off to the Crusades outfitted her with a chastity belt and kept the key with him.

A woman who did not belong to a man, peasant women, and women of questionable reputation were always fair game for rape. These are the type of women who would, because of their inferior moral character, not be worth protecting. Ironically, the word *virgin* comes from the Latin word meaning "strength, force, and skill." It did not refer to sexual chastity but sexual independence. This word has become distorted through biblical translations.

The above mutilative practices, still performed today by some African Muslims, were built on the premise that with an egalitarian order, young girls would merely revert to filthy sex maniacs. Furthermore, they needed to be exploited, punished, and oppressed "for their own good." Women were blamed for everything from their husband's sterility to bad crops, and they were always suspected of being willful seducers of good men. Patriarchy set about judging women for their sexual activity and making them the universal scapegoat for all of life's problems. At the same time, men escaped the terrible burden of questioning themselves.

Patriarchy's reaction to the female cultures that had preceded it was built on many misunderstandings and distortions, but it accounts for much of women's experience with the justice system today. The notion that women are, at their core, evil is seen everywhere, and their truthfulness in rape allegations has always been suspect. As Chief Justice Lord Matthew Hale ruled in the seventeenth century, judges are required to instruct juries, "Rape is an accusation easily to be made, hard to be proved, and harder to be defended by the party accused, though never so innocent" (Brownmiller 1975, 413).

Although Hale's warnings are no longer a part of the court process, rape proceedings are still conducted as if all women tend to lie, or at least become confused about violations of their own body. As our interviews with survivors indicate, today's victim is scrutinized for truthfulness and consistency of detail. Rape laws are designed to protect men from false accusations. Painting a picture of the victim as vengeful or deceitful is still a common courtroom defense tactic, no matter how unfounded. It seems that no one has stopped to consider that rape is reported at a very low rate, lower than assault or burglary, and that it is not an easy accusation to make. Rape laws have protected the majority of rapists, who escape prison sentences.

Patriarchy's version is that women *need* to be owned. Historically, rape has been recognized only as a crime against the male property owner. If the woman who was raped was still the virgin daughter of a father, the law recognized the rape as a crime against the father, whose property was devalued. If the woman was married, the crime was against the husband, whose property was stolen. Rape exposes a woman to the reality that her body may not be her own. Men today still seek to control women's bodies via abortion laws and the promulgation of the rape mythology. In court, a woman who is not married faces more societal censure than one who is married because of the underlying presumption that since no particular man owns her, no party has been wronged. Women who are raped often face rejection by the man with whom they regularly have intercourse, as he may feel that his personal property was defiled. Husbands or partners may reject their wives and accuse them of having enjoyed the sexual contact. Anyone who believes that rape of one's wife or girlfriend doesn't concern ownership hasn't witnessed the incredible rage of a husband who vows to kill the attacker and is angered at police for their apathy.

Most women would wince at the thought of being someone's property. The players have different names now, but laws and procedures have stayed fairly consistent since biblical times. Now rape is prosecuted as a crime against the state, whereas it used to be a crime against the husband's estate. The courtroom is now the venue for pitting two, usually male, adversaries against each other, with the victim as a pawn or trophy to be won. The feeling of being treated as an object in a game is commonly mentioned by women who serve as witnesses in the criminal prosecution of their own rapes. It is not the woman against the rapist but the state, represented by a district attorney, against the rapist. Criminal law still says that a woman's body is not her property when it comes to rape. She must do what the state advises her. She has little or no recourse if she disagrees with the counsel for the state. In addition, the counsel is not even the woman's own attorney. As fate would have it, her alleged attacker does have his own attorney.

John Stoltenberg (1989) writes:

> Patriarchal law both protects and expresses a cultural norm of phallic eroticism. Normally acculturated phallic eroticism responds best and basically to bodies as objects, to human flesh as property. Phallic eroticism is intrinsically proprietorial; it is an eroticism cultivated for owning, and it is dysfunctional and insensate except in relation to human flesh perceived and treated as personal property. . . . Phallic eroticism is intrinsically hostile for violence is necessary to sustain such an unnatural relationship to other human life. By defining men's property rights to the bodies of women, patriarchal law licenses and reinforces each man's private eroticized owning, each man's private eroticized estranging, each man's private eroticized violence. (pp. 62–63)

Stoltenberg's words are telling when it comes to rape prosecution. For instance, the survivor probably holds the view that she does not have the right to defend herself, being that she has not owned her body or sexuality for the past few thousand years. The underlying message for her is that female sexual desirability is defined by our culture as beautiful passivity.

This is a double bind. A jury often will condemn a woman if she did not fight her attacker. It appears that a woman is suddenly supposed to change her personality and become physically aggressive when rape is attempted. More often than not, however, she suffers a paralysis of fear. According to what she has been taught, fighting women are unnatural, undesirable, and laughable. Can you imagine mythic heroines such as Little Red Riding Hood and Snow White garnering the energy to fight the wolf or the wicked witch? They just lie there, tragically immobile, until they are rescued by the huntsman or the prince. A beautiful woman, vulnerable and crumpled on the ground near death, is an acceptable image to men. A powerful woman who claws and scratches is not.

A widely known female radio talk show host has written, "To be truly feminine one must surrender, be receptive and allow life to happen" (Grant 1988, 151). That may be good advice in certain circumstances, but a "feminine attitude" will set a woman up for blame if she is raped. In Mercedes's story (Chapter 5), the survivor did fight off her attacker, and she lost her case because the prosecutor stated, "Had the assailant been able to complete the rape, the jury would probably convict. However, because there were no serious injuries, he was proven not guilty." Women cannot win: if they fight and defend themselves, the crime is minimized; if they are passive and are raped, they are condemned by the jury for not fighting back.

The second area of patriarchal rape mythology that affects a woman who decides to prosecute is whether she knows the attacker. The closer her relationship is to the rapist, the less likely it is that the jury will believe her and the more likely it is that her assailant will claim that she consented. In an ongoing sexual relationship, it's doubtful that a woman would even call an assault rape. Women tend to say that they were forced to have sex when they really didn't want to. In addition, women are told that they are responsible for men's sexual aggressiveness. A woman who is raped may think that others will assume that she seduced him, acquiesced, and then, plagued by moral conflicts, changed her mind afterward. Finally, women have trouble determining whether they are "nice girls" in this age of sexual revolution. In the past, a nice girl was a virgin. Today most women know that they are fair game when out on a date. This may be the most important factor in explaining the low report rate of date rape.

The patriarchal male is a warrior and for this reason is not likely to believe that date rape exists. At first in battle, men learned to band together for the protection of each other. Men support men whom they feel are like them and exhibit great loyalty toward them, something women have forgotten how to do. According to the good old boy syndrome, rapists must be on the enemy's side—a psychopath in the alley with a knife—but certainly not someone like himself. Believing in date rape is like believing that *all* men have the potential to display patriarchal hostility through sexual acts.

Law-abiding men still find rape acceptable under certain conditions. When a man's masculinity is in question, "boys will be boys." In times of war, women are symbols of the enemy. Justification is given for making them a target of rape. Violent acts can be rationalized by calling the enemy's women lascivious or promiscuous. In the Vietnam War, rape was justified because Vietcong women carried weapons. Regardless of how it's condoned, when men are pitted against each other, rape allows them to demonstrate who the real man is, and, like the Greek gods, the conqueror is entitled to the spoils.

The sexual assault of women can even take on overtones of a sporting event. In the movie *The Accused*, a female is raped on a pinball machine while other men stand around and cheer, encouraging their male cohorts to take turns with her body. Amid the spirit of recreation, men affirm male bonding, thus invading and humiliating women in their most private space. Those who fail to go along are ostracized from the group.

The key is expected behavior. We often expect men to rape during the frenzy of war and group violence, but we do not expect rape to occur on a date. The real issue is that rape is an institutionalized crime with a deep-seated underlying philosophy. It is a reenactment of social dominance no matter what the situation, no matter who the target. Its motive is always the subjugation of another human being for economic and psychological gain. The appearance of rape in the social history of the world makes it part of the unspoken fabric of modern existence. Whether we refer to the rape of black slaves during the Civil War or the literature of pornography, rape is part of our patriarchal heritage. This form of social dominance feeds the ego of the aggressor, subverts the ego of the victim, and corrupts healthy sexuality by destroying the mutuality of consent.

Rape demonstrates contempt for the other, bolstered by distrust. According to Susan Brownmiller (1975), "Rapists may also operate within an emotional setting or within a dependent relationship that provides a hierarchical, authoritarian structure of its own that weakens a victim's resistance, distorts her perspective and confounds her will" (p. 213).

Rape turns people into objects. In a variety of scenarios, people act out power roles in which the young, the weak, or the dependent become prey. Men can be raped, although this is rarely mentioned. In prison, the authorities tolerate, and perhaps even encourage, homosexual rape. The scapegoat in prison rapes is often the effeminate, slightly built youth who becomes the woman. He represents the beauty, pain, and passivity synonymous with femininity, which the aggressor finds attractive. In the sexual abuse of a child, whether perpetrated by a stranger or a family member, the child's vulnerability is exploited by the authoritarian adult-child structure. In spousal rape, a woman financially dependent on her husband must tolerate his physical coercion. In all of these instances, the victim is blamed: "The faggot deserved it"; "The child seduced me"; "She owes it to me."

In a dating situation, we do not usually think of an authoritarian structure. Direct confrontation falls outside the behavioral norms, and it is assumed that the two people are of equal power. Yet the dynamics of date rape follow the abuse of power patterns set forth above. A man gives a woman a gift and expects repayment. This is the power hierarchy. Sometimes the gift is dinner; sometimes it's merely flattery and attention. Both incest and date rape depict the abuse of power by a person you least expect will betray you. The victim wants to believe he or she is liked, if not loved, by the oppressor. In both instances, the victim becomes convinced that he or she is an accomplice to the crime and takes on deep feelings of guilt and shame. Date rape, like child sexual abuse, can occur in all socioeconomic classes.

We can think of no more potentially destructive abuse of authoritarian power than by the conditions set up once a rape is reported.

Police and district attorneys have a psychological edge that lessens any need for physical coercion merely because they are in the role of helper. Because of the victim's vulnerability, and the trust and respect we are taught for these professions, they in particular can weaken her resistance, distort her perspective, and confound her will before she even realizes her predicament. Because of these professionals' aura of rightness, their actions cannot be easily challenged. Recall that the motive of rape is humiliation and degradation. It can occur in a nonphysical way.

What is the current status of patriarchal oppression as humankind enters the 1990s? By now all of us are accustomed to industries that exist and profit solely by momentary diversions from the realization that we are still on the wrong path. Patriarchy has become sneakier. It offers us drugs, alcohol, the entertainment media, fashion, cosmetics, pornography, drive-in sermons, and a pace of life that leaves us little time to think about what is occurring. Patriarchal institutions are the remedy for all the "quietly desperate people seeking an anesthetic escape from the pain of personal alienation" (Sjöö and Mor 1987, 29). The spiritual male and female of a long-gone age are repressed by keeping this alienating institution alive and intact. Meanwhile, humankind continues to exploit more than ever mother earth, as well as the mother goddess who united us with ourselves, with each other, and with nature.

The institution of rape occurs against a backdrop of sexual violence that pervades our culture in both obvious and subtle forms. The pairing of sex and violence is reflected in our mythic heroes. Don Juan is idealized as the greatest seducer of Spain. Aggression, hate, and desire to humiliate and punish women are Don Juan's underlying motives. Today many rock groups build their careers on simulated onstage abuse of women for autoerotic thrills. Music videos pair sex and violence against women. The most radical degradation of women are the snuff movies, in which women are sexually abused and then finally murdered. Society pays a great deal of money to read and hear attitudes that promote the despoiling and degradation of women. It would seem that patriarchal institutions are trying harder than ever to condition us to accept violence toward women, no matter what we may consciously profess. These are the ingrained myths and attitudes that every defense attorney plays on with the jury.

Society further force-feeds contradiction and confusion to women. Young women are encouraged to dress provocatively, with short skirts and string bikinis. Men want attractive, seductive women. But when women are raped or murdered, men say, "This is what happens to women who try to seduce men." Patriarchy is still making women into the evil goddess or witch and burning them at the stake.

What is the current status of women? Women have a legacy of rising above the suppression of their gender. The feminist movement of the nineteenth century freed women from oppressive forms of male dominance. Like the nineteenth-century feminist movement, the women's movement that began in the 1960s also has improved the situation for women. This movement has pressed for new laws to protect women both inside and outside the home. Modern feminism has upgraded the situation of women and men by raising people's consciousness about activities that were once under male control.

Unfortunately, by the time a sizable number of women forcefully demand or achieve any gains, a backlash of male dominance is generally already under way. As historian Theodore Roszak notes, the resistance to the nineteenth-century feminist movement was marked by an increase in aggravated assault and domestic beating by males (Eisler 1987).

During the counterculture movement of the 1960s and 1970s, young men challenged the conception of warfare as heroic and manly and began switching to more effeminate styles of dress and hair, and women were making important gains in equal rights. But at the same time, old sexual stereotypes challenged these advances, and the forces of the conservative movement were well at hand. A male backlash was gathering steam in opposition to the Equal Rights Amendment (ERA) and in support of the Moral Majority and other right-wing groups (Eisler 1987).

Whenever feminist values have gained popularity for a time, threatening to transform the system, an aroused and fearful male faction has squelched them. In the wake of the twentieth-century women's movement has come a substantial rise in violence against women. Roszak gives examples such as Indian bride burnings, Iranian public executions, Latin American imprisonment and torture, and worldwide wife battering (Eisler 1987). The global terrorism of rape, which scholars estimate now occurs in the United States at the rate of one every thirteen seconds (Eisler 1987), also is prevalent. It appears that the message to women is "Stay in your subservient role and keep quiet about inequality, or you will be punished!"

Speaking up and fighting back after a rape requires great courage. Most survivors, particularly those who survive date rape, never report or talk about it. Most rapists count on silence. Pressure and humiliation is often forced on the survivor so that she will drop the charges. Women have always understood the political implications of a public admission of rape. Since biblical times, women have anticipated, justifiably, that only further shame and degradation will follow. It is little wonder that some survivors choose to punish their assaulters themselves.

As Natalie Shainess (1984) says in her book *Sweet Suffering: Woman as Victim,* women are trained to be rape victims. Vulnerability is still a prized female trait. Some of our greatest thinkers, such as Helen Deutch and Sigmund Freud, referred to masochism as the natural or preferred state of all women. Pain is women's due. If that is so, the survivors whose stories are related in the following chapters have certainly exemplified their gender's ultimate quintessence. Their stories, however, bear no resemblance to storybook romances or pornographic fantasies. They are real.

Before we met Lydia, a woman brutally raped by a stranger, we pictured a tough, crass woman. Who else would tend bar in one of the sleeziest parts of town? This bar was known for the brawls that occurred outside just after closing. It catered to Hispanics, so we even thought we might encounter a cultural or language barrier in understanding her. Instead we were surprised to meet an Anglo woman with a short, sophisticated hairstyle and conservative clothing. She was a homemaker and seamstress, and she definitely didn't fit our stereotype of a female bartender. She was not flamboyant, provocative, loud, or sexy, nor was she an alcoholic. She was a forty-seven-year-old single mother who had just relocated to a new town. She was in real estate, and the bartending job was temporary until the profits of her real estate job began to pay off. Being new in the area, she was unaware of the bar's reputation.

Debbie, another survivor, did not know that the club where she went had a reputation for its crystal (methamphetamine) clientele. Like Lydia, she was conservative in her manner and dress. Nothing set her apart from any other woman her age except that she looked and acted more like the proverbial girl next door than most. She also had the courage to prosecute her rapist for an acquaintance rape—which most women do not.

Mercedes, a teenager, successfully fought off her attacker and chose to prosecute him. She was attractive, feminine, and vulnerable, but she was skilled in defending herself.

Katie was a compliant young woman who hoped that the military would give her opportunity, training, and self-esteem. Instead, she gave in to her male superior ("Rank has its privileges") and was raped. Her high hopes soon turned into nightmare and disillusionment.

Poor Red, perhaps the most tragic of all survivors, was the most successful in maintaining the desirable feminine attitude. She didn't make waves; she surrendered, was receptive, and allowed life to happen. Even this stance, however, would be judged today. Because she didn't fight, she also would be blamed.

We have a long way to go to change our attitudes toward rape. We hope that this book will be one vehicle for that change. As French philosopher Charles Fourier observed, "The degree of emancipation of women is an index of the degree of society's emancipation" (Eisler 1987, 150).

# PART TWO

# The Survivors

# 3

# Lydia's Story: Stranger Rape

I was new in town and trying to make it in real estate. We all know how long that can take, so I decided to take a second job bartending. I wasn't wild about taking a second job, especially bartending, but as a single parent, in the past it had put a few groceries on the table when times were tough.

When I was hired for the job, the owner of the bar explained that things could get a little rough, but I didn't have any doubts about being able to handle it. I have always been a strong person and never considered myself a wimp in any way. The owner also told me that a lot of the customers were Hispanic. That didn't bother me either. I felt like I was probably the most unprejudiced person alive. You see, I had this love for all human beings. I guess, looking back on it, I was pretty naive, but I just never thought I'd get hurt. I have always taken pride in treating everyone with kindness and respect. I mean, after all, I had surmounted unbelievable odds in my life—a real crazy family and two abusive marriages. So at this time of my life, I felt so strong that I thought I was invincible.

Anyway, those first few weeks at the bar went great. I made friends with so many of the patrons. Many of the men were nice to me and really protective if anyone tried to give me a hard time. I was even asked to shoot pool with them, so I knew I was in.

One night a couple of guys started to come into the bar with open bottles of beer. I went over and reminded them of the rule about no open beer bottles. One guy argued with me a lot, but they both finally dropped the bottles outside and came on in. I heard one of them mumble something hateful under his breath.

When it was closing time and I asked everyone to leave, I noticed that these same two guys were kind of hanging around. Again, I had to use my firm voice to get my point across, but they finally went out the door. Just as I was going over to lock it, they came back inside. They locked the door behind them, and I got mad because I thought they were probably going to steal the money that we had made that night. Well, I decided that I wasn't going to give up that money without a fight. I ran for the telephone, but one guy ripped the cord from the wall. The other guy got into the register and was taking the money. It began to dawn on me that only one guy was after the money and the other guy was trying to grab me. He tore at my clothes and said, "This is your life, white bitch!" I picked up a beer bottle and hit him on the head. The bottle broke. It didn't even phase him, but it sure made him mad. He had me on the floor, with the jagged beer bottle at my neck, when the guy with the money just stepped over us and walked out. I begged and pleaded with him to help me, but he just kept going and didn't look back.

The man who was doing this to me seemed to know exactly what he was doing, like he had done it millions of times before. It was as if he had a method or routine. He took the jagged beer bottle and cut off my clothes. When he took an upward sweep at my bra, I thought the bottle would jab into my neck and I would die. Luckily, he caught the elastic of my bra instead of my neck. It seemed like the more terrified I got, the more he liked what he was doing.

He took some matches and set my pubic hairs on fire. All the time, I was pleading with him not to do this to me. When he discovered I was having my period and had a tampon, he removed the tampon and tried to enter me. He then tried to put his penis in my mouth, but I pretended my jaw was broken from his struggle with me. He kept cussing at me—calling me cunt and whore and saying, "Your life is over, white bitch."

He wrote graffiti all over my body with black magic marker, and he did everything so methodically, like this wasn't his first time. I really believed he meant to kill me, because I will never forget the look in his eyes. His eyes were cold and vacant as if he had no soul. I kept pleading with him to let me go, but he kept on and on with the torture. I later found out the ordeal had lasted for two hours.

Next I did something that I believe saved my life. I don't know where the thought came from, but I pretended to be unconscious. I let my whole body go limp. The rapist lifted my hand and arm, and let it drop loosely at my side. When he was sure I was unconscious, he went into the bathroom. I really don't know why he went in there. I don't think he had come one time while he was raping me, so maybe he went in there to do it himself. Anyway, I decided this might be my only chance to escape, so I got up and bolted for the door. Just as I got to the door, he came out of the bathroom and saw me. I was shaking so much that I couldn't get the door unlocked. I must have been turning the lock the wrong way even though I had locked and unlocked it a hundred times. His hand was only inches from my shoulder when I finally got the door open.

I was running naked down the street at 3 A.M., with blood and urine streaming down my legs. I never took the time to look back, but he must have been afraid to chase me because there was another man outside on the street. I thought the man on the street might be a friend of the rapist's, so I ran the other way. I was screaming, crying, and yelling "help." I remembered that the police station was nearby, so I ran there. It was totally dark, though, and the door was locked. A man on the street yelled at me, but I was afraid of him, too. When he took off his trousers and threw them at me, I realized that he was trying to help. Someone must have heard me yelling because soon there were three police cars.

I was interviewed by one of the policemen. I was hysterical and probably in shock, but he was kind and gentle. I wish he had tape-recorded that initial interview because I think he wrote some things down wrong. I don't remember much of what I said. He took me to the hospital, and that was horrible. The last thing I wanted was to have someone else poke and prod at my body. The hospital wanted to take pictures of my body, but I was so humiliated by the shape I was in that I just couldn't let them. I was so bloody and stained with urine. It was just so degrading for anyone to see what was written all over me in magic marker. I scrubbed and scrubbed, but that marker would just not come off for days.

The nurses were very sympathetic and kind, but the doctor who examined me acted irritated that he had to do the examination. He didn't know how to talk with me, and he acted like he didn't know what he was doing. Because I was hysterical and angry about being raped, he offered me Valium. I yelled at him then and said, "No, I don't want Valium! I'm depressed enough without taking a downer." I felt as if his message to me was to take a pill and calm down.

A police investigator came to see me that night at the hospital, and he was sensitive enough not to put me through more questions. He said he could come over to my home within a few days. I remember that I was obsessed with getting my car home, so the police investigator took me home that night and made sure he got my car home, too.

I was so scared in those weeks following the rape. Feeling fear was new to me, and I hated it. I was a woman who had always driven alone at night on the freeway, never believing that anything could happen to me. But now I was afraid to leave my home and slept on the couch so I could hear any sound coming near the front door. I kept going over and over the rape in my mind, wishing I had jammed my fingers into his eyes. He was still out there somewhere. I wished that I had been able to kill him. The extent of my anger scared me. Never in my life had I felt such hate for another human being. I had dreams of killing him. I kept seeing those vacant, cold eyes.

On several nights, I called the rape crisis hot line at 1 or 2 A.M. just to talk for an hour or two. The counselors reassured me that feelings of hate and fear were normal. I had such feelings of guilt over my fantasies of brutalizing the rapist.

I kept remembering more details of the rape and called the police repeatedly. Most of the time, it appeared that they were uninterested in what I had to say, and I believe they were only pretending to conduct an investigation. For example, I wanted them to take fingerprints of items on the bar. They assured me that that was standard procedure and had been done. Later, however, I found out that no prints had been taken.

The police were certain that the offenders were on the other side of the border; something in my gut told me otherwise. I became obsessed with catching them. I really feel that if it hadn't been for my prodding of the police and my determination, they would have eventually killed me. I felt that the rapist had to be behind bars, or

I would never rest again. I didn't feel as angry at the thief as I did at the rapist, but I wondered how he could have ignored my cry for his help, just stepping over me while his friend was brutalizing me.

Tasks that were simple before became terrifying experiences. A trip to the grocery store was almost impossible for me. Each time I saw a Hispanic male, I began shaking. I continually checked behind me to make sure no one was following. I had to quit my real estate job because each time I tried to go someplace alone, to unknown territory, I became nauseated and had to throw up.

What bothered me most was that my entire way of living was turned upside down. After the rape, I changed from a woman who feared nothing to one who feared everything.

I kept phoning the police to tell them I knew those men were still in town. Still, the police were sure that I was just a hysterical woman. I even got a telephone call from one of my coworkers at the bar who said he was sure the same two men had come back into the bar to shoot pool and drink. I decided I would have to take things into my own hands. I cut my hair and frosted it, put on sunglasses, and went back to the bar myself. I was so angry about so many things. The nerve of those guys to come back to the same bar! The apathy of the police was infuriating to me.

A few days later, I got a call from the police saying they thought they had caught the rapist. He had come back to the bar, and a coworker had called them. I learned later that before the police got there, some of the patrons had roughed him up a bit. And for many months afterward, when I was afraid that justice wouldn't be done, I wished they or I had killed him and never called the police.

The police wanted me to identify the rapist from a lineup of men. I knew immediately who he was—it was those eyes. I kept thinking, "What if he escapes from jail or his friends get him out—I'm dead!" Still, it was some comfort to know that he was behind bars.

I took an active role in catching the other guy, the thief. A bartender called me one night and said he thought the second guy was there, shooting pool. As I drove to the bar, I felt fear, dread, and excitement at finally apprehending both men. I walked in and recognized him immediately, but he didn't even look up. I went into the back room and called the police. As I was waiting for the police to come, I broke out in a cold sweat. My knees got weak, and I had to sit down, or I would have fallen down, remembering the events of that night.

When the police came and took the thief away, there was remorse on his face. It's hard to believe, but I felt some pity for him. Later, during the court proceedings, the judge sentenced him to four years in prison, and I felt that was a fair punishment.

The preliminary hearing was one month later. I was making it through that day pretty well until the prosecuting attorney made the rapist take off his shirt. That was so I could identify some acne-type scars on his back. When I saw his back at close range, I was flooded with memories and thought for sure I was going to throw up.

I soon began to realize that I didn't have the right to have an attorney on my behalf. The prosecuting attorney, who I first thought was my attorney, was actually representing the state in which I live. I felt totally ignored by him. I tried to call him many times, but he just ignored me. The corker came the day I got an impersonal letter from him stating that they had bargained about my assaulter's sentence. I just about came unglued. How dare he decide that this was okay with me! I, the victim of the crime, was not even asked for my opinion. I felt let down that there would not be a trial by jury. I wanted him to get the maximum sentence. When I was finally able to reach the district attorney, I told him how furious I was. He tried to placate me by saying, "Rape cases are hard to win, and this is a really fair bargain. It's the best you can expect, and the trial would be hard on you." After that day, he ignored me more than ever. I guess women aren't supposed to get mad.

Because the preliminary hearing was so upsetting for me, my psychologist came with me for each sentencing after. I spent many sleepless nights preparing a statement to explain how I felt to the judge and rapist. At the next court date, however, sentencing did not occur. The judge postponed it due to an incomplete psychological evaluation of my attacker. All this attention given to the legal rights of the rapist just blew my mind. He also wanted to change his plea to one of consensual sex. I was furious. I suppose people generally burn their lover's pubic hair while making love! I could feel myself boiling inside. When the rapist was asked if he was satisfied with his representation by his defense attorney, he said yes.

One month later, I again went to sentencing. I was feeling so happy that at last this whole thing would be over. Surely by now they had everything they needed. I kept looking for the prosecuting attorney, but he was nowhere in sight. I began to panic and then felt furious. It became obvious that everyone in the courtroom except my psychologist and me knew that sentencing would be postponed again. "Why wasn't I told?" I thought. "I am the victim of this crime, and everyone treats me like I don't even exist." I really fumed when the prosecuting attorney did not bother to speak to me that morning as he stuck his head inside the courtroom. I felt so abandoned and ignored that I ran from the room and threw up.

The postponement was due to the rapist's request for a different defense attorney. I couldn't believe it. Just four weeks earlier, he had said he was satisfied with his attorney. I'm sure they wouldn't even have considered giving me a new district attorney, although I was getting more dissatisfied by the minute.

As I left the courtroom that day, I was disillusioned and disappointed. I was disillusioned that the legal system gave him more rights and consideration than it gave me. And I was disappointed that the sentencing was postponed two more months and I would have to go through Christmas with nothing resolved. Most of all, I was furious that the prosecuting attorney had not had the consideration to call me. The person designated to represent the people of the state was treating me like a nobody.

I also felt panic as I looked at this man who had no remorse in his eyes. I had believed that I would be protected by our legal system. Now the reality hit me that I was still vulnerable, alone, and afraid. "If he's so clever to stall like this," I thought, "will he escape or collude with some of his friends on the outside to silence me forever?" What had happened to the strong Lydia? Where had she gone?

On the day of the final sentencing in January, I really didn't believe it would happen. I had had a migraine headache for two days, and I didn't feel ready to give my statement that day in the courtroom. My enthusiasm and trust in justice had dwindled.

I'm lucky, though, because that day in January, some of my faith in human beings was restored. On that day, as I stood up to give my statement to the judge and my attacker, my voice was quaking and I had tears in my eyes, but I did get my message across. My message was that he would have to pay for his crime and that he had chosen the wrong person as his victim, since I had been strong enough to see this ordeal through. I felt that I owed it to my fellow men and women not to allow this person to be in society, where he would probably kill or rape others.

When I finished my statement, there was not a dry eye in the courtroom, including the judge's. The judge gave the rapist the maximum sentence of twenty-four years. He said that only an animal could be so brutal. Still, there was no look of remorse in the rapist's eyes.

My biggest reward that day did not come from the sentence the rapist got but from a totally unexpected gesture by the defense attorney. After the hearing, the defense attorney, who was a Hispanic male, walked up to me and handed me a Bible. He had tears in his eyes and didn't know what to say. He didn't have to say anything because the look between us said it all. The look he gave me said, "Please forgive this one man for his hatred and violence and not condemn us all."

Since that time, I have returned the Bible to the defense attorney. It was too precious a gift to keep, as it was handed down to him from his grandfather. I let him know that his gesture was one of the most important factors in my recovery.

Most days I think I'm going to be okay. I'm having a hard time regaining my confidence to go back to work because the old Lydia is gone and I don't know who the new Lydia is yet. Maybe I was too trusting before. I'm more careful now. It's sad to have to be on guard just because I'm female.

## Authors' Commentary

One cannot read Lydia's story without admiring her strength. She is a woman with incredible courage and stamina.

It is apparent that her rape was a violent one—so violent that she felt her own death was imminent. And yet she did what is atypical for most women: she fought back and escaped.

After the rape, she felt something within her that she had never experienced: a paralyzing fear of her attacker and rage toward him. She felt as if the old Lydia, with confidence, faith, and trust in human beings, was gone. What was worse, she felt guilty about the new Lydia, who was vulnerable, fearful, and angry.

As time passed, the old Lydia resurfaced. She kept calling the police, prodding them to catch her assailant and his accomplice. Even though stranger rape is the preferred category of rape for police involvement, Lydia felt that she had to prod the police to act. She even disguised herself so she could be active in her assailant's capture.

It became obvious to Lydia that she was more assertive than most survivors when the district attorney wanted her to back off and leave everything in his hands. In fact, he ignored her on several occasions. The underlying message to her was that good victims and women aren't supposed to question police or legal proceedings, and they especially aren't supposed to get angry. Many police personnel and district attorneys think that women are unfairly directing their anger at them when they are really angry at the rapist.

As far as the crime of rape, Lydia was fortunate in several ways. First, she was alive. She was strong enough and had enough determination to weather the legal process through all the delays and disappointments. She was fortunate that her attacker was a stranger. According to Estrich (1987), rapes by strangers are the type most likely to be won in court. She had significant physical injuries and thus evidence that she had struggled. She also saw her attacker receive a sentence of twenty-four years, which is substantial for a rapist.

One and a half years after the rape, Lydia is making great strides. She no longer trembles at the approach of every male. She is starting to feel confident and has just received a job promotion. Unfortunately, the rape is something she will never forget. But she exemplifies the meaning of the word *survivor*.

# 4

# Debbie's Story: Date Rape

I guess from the beginning it was really bad for me that I met Jim in a nightclub. Actually, I had never been to a club alone before, but I was new in town and didn't know a soul. I'd recently separated from my husband and wasn't dating. To be honest, I was lonely.

I thought I'd found somebody really special when Jim approached me at the Oar House. I was so happy to have the company of such a nice guy. He was twenty-five, one year older than myself, clean-cut, so handsome in his stone-washed jeans and Reebok tennies. His hair was perfect; he was meticulously clean—not at all the scum a woman worries about attracting in a place like that.

Not only did he look like the boy next door, but he had a cute smile, and we laughed and laughed. Everything was fun and exciting that first night; he was a great dancer. I was kind of cautious, though, and I thought, "He'll make a great date, but I don't really know him." In fact, all the warning signals were going off, so in the beginning, I wouldn't even give him my phone number but took his. Well, actually . . . we had sex the first night at his place. We started making out in the parking lot. This is really embarrassing . . . but I liked that he held me afterward and we fell asleep in each other's arms.

Jim told me that he was living in a motel, trying to get the deposit money together for an apartment. He said he'd gotten mad at his former girlfriend for having an abortion and had packed up and left. He never really mentioned any friends or family. All this time

I thought he was going to work each day. He said he worked temporarily for a moving company.

Two weeks of great dating followed—laughing, tickling, jokes. Jim was such a happy person; he was so great. Then one night he called me, violently ill, from his motel room. He was having an ulcer attack and vomiting blood. I felt very sorry for him. He also had no money left for the motel room, so I invited him to stay with me— just for two weeks—so that he could get back on his feet. I guess, in the back of my mind, I reasoned that he would repay my kindness by being nice to me and not leaving me. During that time, I also financially supported him with my job as an accounting clerk in my family's business and my job as a part-time model.

After two months, he was still there. I started to feel really betrayed. He wasn't living up to his end of the deal. I kept asking him to get a job and find a place of his own, but, well, by this time I realized he had some real mental problems. By the time I threw his things out for the first time, I had discovered he was a crystal (methamphetamine) freak. I guess that a lot of drug users hang out in that club. I didn't know. So even though he had this addiction and I caught herpes from him, I still felt I could change him. He had a way of making me feel sorry for him so that I would do whatever he wanted. He was very manipulative.

Jim stayed in my apartment house but moved across the hall. It seemed we spent most of our time together in violent arguments. He was obsessively jealous. He would abruptly stop the fights at the most dangerous time and hug me, saying, "It's okay, honey." Then he'd want to have sex to make up. My initial attraction to him was physical; his primary ability was sexual. I was molested by my stepdad when I was a child. Sex to me was love.

Eventually, I told Jim he needed to get help for his problems. All the time I saw him talking out the window to people who weren't there. Then he told me that God was talking to him through the radio. He said he'd go see a counselor if I would just stand by him. I let him move back in because, again, he had no place to live. One time he did actually quit the drugs for five days. During the withdrawal, he started reading Bible verses about death. He'd sit for eight hours on the hill above my apartment and watch me. He followed me wherever I went.

Meanwhile, things were getting more violent. I'd get provoked; there was lots of hitting and screaming. I thought to myself, "I've lost control; what am I doing?" This emotional intensity went on for four months. He'd keep me up talking all night. I wasn't sleeping or eating; I was isolated from all outside contact and communication. I guess you could say I was brainwashed. At any rate, I didn't even recognize myself.

Eventually, I pulled myself together and for the second time threw out his belongings. This time I had the locks changed. I started to go out again. At that point, I was no longer attracted to him. He would come by every day or so. I'd open the door, and he'd just stare at me, not saying anything. I knew he was watching my apartment and every move I made. He described my dates with friends in detail. I was just trying to get away from him. I didn't see Jim as dangerous, even though one time he told me he was going to kill his former girlfriend. I thought he was just immature and a real crystal freak.

It never occurred to me to call the police for my own protection. I just kept begging him to get help. He'd punch himself in the face; he became suicidal and begged me to kill him. I finally dragged him to the Veterans Administration (VA) hospital and asked them for inpatient care for Jim. They turned us away with a pamphlet on Narcotics Anonymous (NA). He said he'd go if I went with him. I did. I also told him that I'd let him move back if he went to NA and stopped using. He was clean for one and a half months, and I thought everything was going to be fine. He still had mood swings, but they were less extreme. He still didn't have a job, but I thought maybe in a few years he would be normal; maybe we could be friends then.

The crisis started on my twenty-fifth birthday. He still was not using but got enraged with me because he said I wasn't paying attention to him at my party. I had left the party with a girlfriend for a short time, and when I returned, he shouted, "Where the fuck have you been?" That night he started using again, and for the third time I threw him out. I told him this time I never wanted to see him again. I knew for certain he was really sick. I guess he was living in his car, but I no longer cared about helping him. This time, fortunately, he didn't have a key.

Two days later, I came home tired from work. I opened my door to find Jim sitting in my living room, slumped over in a chair. I could only think of how tired and powerless I was. He told me the maintenance man had let him in. I asked him to leave, went into the bedroom, and went to sleep. I had no energy left to get mad at him. In fact, by this time I didn't think I had any rights; I felt totally defeated. I could only get some rest and go to work tomorrow. He left me alone.

The next night when I came home from work, he was still there. This time he entered the bedroom. I was reading a book in bed in my flannel pajamas. He got into my bed and repeatedly tried to rip my underwear off. I kept screaming no and ran into the bathroom. He was right behind me. He slammed me into a counter and attempted to choke me and punch me in the head. I knew he was on drugs. I thought of running down the hall out my door, but he had me trapped. I'm not very big—only five feet five inches. He then threw me from the doorway of the bedroom onto the bed. I was scared to death! He tore my clothes off and tried to enter me vaginally but couldn't do it. I was too dry. Then he tried anally. I thought, "He's hurting me, and now he wants to have sex with me." Violence, then a hug; throwing me around, then making up. Same old pattern—I didn't think it was rape.

For hours, it seemed, he slammed my uterus with what felt like a baseball bat. I lay there, not looking at him, not fighting, passive. He had my ankles held back over my head. All the time he kept saying, "I'm punishing you because you've been a bad girl. I'm giving it to you for every time you've screwed someone."

The punishment lasted for five hours. At the end, I was in serious pain. I tried kicking him in the face, but mostly I was scared. I was concerned about the integrity of my body. I felt like he was ripping me from inside out. I had ripping, searing pain—the most severe pain I've ever felt. I was sobbing uncontrollably. While he was doing it, I kept thinking of stories he'd told me about his childhood—the mother who'd forced him to put his hand in hot boiling fudge as a punishment and the foster mother who had slammed a dildo into his anus as punishment. At times he would talk in what I called his devil voice, saying, "I'm going to kill you; you're a bad girl."

I can't remember Jim ejaculating, but eventually he pushed me over in the middle of the bed and started hugging me. He said, "I'm going to marry you. Everything will be okay." He tried to comfort me, calm me down. I wouldn't let him. It was still hard to think of this as rape, although I knew I had never in a million years submitted willingly to the anal entry.

In response, like the night before, I focused on what I needed to do to keep functioning. I had a fashion show to get ready for that started in forty-five minutes. I wasn't thinking of how my behavior would later look to a jury. As I got up to get ready, I said, "You are so fucking crazy." It was now late evening, about 10 P.M.; he wouldn't let me shower by myself. He always took so long showering, I got out before him. I told him I had to get dressed. I got ready for work quickly and tiptoed down the hall to make my escape. I felt tremendous fear, like I'd been captured and held prisoner in my own home. I shot for the door and ran for my car. It never occurred to me to call the police. My plan was to go from the fashion show to my family's home, where I'd find safety.

During my modeling that night, I didn't think about what had happened. I thought, "I'll think of it tomorrow." But then I looked out in the audience and saw him. The fear started all over again. How had he gotten in uninvited? How had he known where I would be? Then I remembered he'd been following me for several months. I thought, "I need some lead time, or he'll follow me and kill me."

Actually, I didn't go to my parents' house as I'd planned. I guess I didn't want them to see the craziness or degradation I'd gotten involved in. I chose the appropriate over the safe; I went home to my apartment. I thought, "He's never going away, but he had enough earlier. He'll leave me alone." I was wrong.

It started all over again almost the minute I went in. He was behind me. There really wasn't any point in locking him out; he'd proven he could get to me if he wanted to. Again, I felt like an animal fighting for my life. He pinned me down for three hours and assaulted me. This time I screamed hysterically, hoping the guys upstairs would hear me. That's when he wasn't sticking a pillow over my face and telling me he was going to kill me. He told me he would break my neck if I didn't shut up. I was more worried about the physical than the sexual abuse. He kept punching my forehead.

I was screaming and crying so loudly for help and for him to stop that I had a panic attack and thought I was dying of a heart attack. The most frightening point was when I realized the neighbors wouldn't help. I know they heard me.

The funny thing is that there was a loaded gun wedged under the mattress of the bed we were on. He kept asking me to kill him. Then I told him I would go and get the gun. He thought it was across the room. When he released me to get the gun, I walked to the other room and dialed 911.

Jim said the police didn't scare him and he'd be back for me. When two patrolmen arrived at my door shortly thereafter, he walked out to meet them. I guess I was expecting at least one female officer. I gave my account and asked that he be locked up. Jim explained his scratch marks by saying I was just a hysterical bitch. I never actually told the patrolmen that I'd been raped. I said, "He's forced himself on me." I thought rape was when you didn't know the person. One said, "You want to prosecute for rape?" in a condescending tone of voice. I told him no because it was evident that even he didn't believe me. They asked Jim to leave and said, "He won't bother you again." Sure; they didn't know how persistent he was.

When I got home the next day, I found weird messages on my answering machine from Jim, although he didn't identify himself. Reese's Peanut Butter Cup wrappers and beer cans were strewn all over, evidence that he had been there. My handgun also was gone. I called the police again. By this time, I had washed and destroyed all the physical evidence. I was told by the patrolman who came out that I couldn't press charges and most women don't follow through. He said I had one hour to prosecute and that it was department policy. Fortunately, I had called my brother-in-law, a law enforcement officer in another county. He had told me that it was rape and that I should keep trying to prosecute.

On the third day, while I was at my parents' house, Jim showed up to see me. He acted like nothing had happened. I called 911 again. Two deputies came out, but by the time they got there, he was gone. I told them what had happened since the initial report, and they couldn't believe that nothing had been done. When I repeated what the former one had said about one hour to prosecute, this one said, "That's a lie." They called the department and put me in touch with a special investigator; his name was Detective Moore. When he came out to talk with me, he said, "You were right to call; you've been hurt." At last I felt hope.

Together we worked to locate Jim. We staked out a friend's apartment and found him. I located a witness, an ex-girlfriend to whom he'd done the same thing. This is the one he wanted to kill. She had had him arrested two times but in the end refused to press charges. Therefore, Jim was a first-time offender. When questioned by the investigator, Jim told five different accounts of those two nights of horror. The district attorney said I didn't have much ammunition. We were dependent on his confession. After four hours, Detective Moore received a confession to five counts, among them sodomy, rape, assault, and theft of a handgun. Without it, I was told, I didn't have a chance of prosecuting.

Jim's defense was that I had just gotten tired of him so was screaming rape when I'd actually consented. Despite the fact that he eventually confessed, I was informed that they had bargained about the sentence. I was told he had pled guilty to rape.

It took four months of appearances, reappearances, and postponements to receive the final sentencing. Throughout I was hoping Jim would get mental health treatment, so a psychological evaluation was ordered at my insistence. I was never allowed to read it, and I don't even know who the doctor was. On the final day of sentencing, I found out that this psychiatrist had said Jim wasn't dangerous. The doctor never interviewed me and could not have known of his threats to kill me or of his childhood history of brutal abuse.

The defense attorney said, "She just picks up on men, and when she gets tired of them, she just throws them away." Much of the talk at sentencing involved my moral character—after he had already confessed. Nobody informed me that I could speak on my behalf and could have defended myself each time the defense attorney spoke. I just sat there quietly and took it. In the end, Jim received a total jail term of 270 days. He had already served half of that time and had three weeks left to serve before he'd be off on good behavior. He also received five years' probation and drug rehabilitation counseling as a sentence. The only thing that changed due to my efforts at the sentencing was that probation was extended from two years to five years. I also found out at the sentencing that Jim had pled guilty to intent to commit rape and that was the only count that will ever show on his record.

I felt really let down by those I thought would help. I felt further degradation. I was even told by a victim's aid program that I probably wasn't qualified for victim's compensation for my medical or therapy expenses. I got therapy anyway, although I paid for it myself. I felt as degraded by the two sets of patrolmen as by the attacker. I felt that a lot of people thought I was dirty, that I'd been to bed with him before and, therefore, I'd take him back. It was like I had no right to press charges.

But I've learned a lot about myself from my therapy. Like most women, I thought rape was something that would never happen to me. I was raised with upper-middle-class values. I had never been physically abused. Rape was, I thought, caused by the way you lived. I bought the myth that it only happens to certain lower-class trashy women who ask for it. I could not think of myself as being raped even when it was occurring. In fact, I didn't think of myself as a victim of a criminal act, and that's why I didn't get help for so long. That hurt my case. I look and act like your sister, your niece, your daughter, your granddaughter, your next-door neighbor. I'm not an ugly person, and I hate to say it, but that's why I thought I wouldn't be believed.

I've also learned about my codependency. It's not really a sickness; it's just that part of being female that gets you in trouble if you aren't so lucky. Codependency is enabling someone else in a relationship with you to be dependent. But then I'd been raised to be that way: to be kind, helpful, generous, and concerned about others' feelings. After all, that's all it started as—just me helping a person in need because of his medical, psychological, and financial problems. I'd been indicted for my kindness. You want to know the worst rape? It's of my values by a society that says women are supposed to be this way and then when they get hurt and suffer, blames them for not behaving like a man. Jim *and* society have exploited my goodness, my trust, and my femaleness.

I've come to understand Jim as well and what the attraction was. He was an addict—not just to drugs but to sex, with me as the object. In retrospect I can see a lot of the signs. Sure I should have known that the Oar House was a crystal hangout. I should have known what "Do you party?" meant when one of his acquaintances asked me in the first few weeks. I should have known that his inability to get a full erection in the beginning is commonly referred to as "crystal dick." Jim is a con man; he was practicing picking up women and having them support him. I remember thinking, "Bud, you're working at this." He lived like he was acting in a play, even looked like a young boy (he didn't have hair on his chest). He spent hours on his public appearance. But then I can't blame myself too much for not recognizing his dangerousness. Even a specialist didn't see his true colors. He's just a normal, likable, all-American boy who made a little mistake (attempted rape?) by taking some drugs. You know, he is the most dangerous rapist of all—the nice guy.

## Two Months Later

People have been telling me all along that Jim will never bother me again. A while ago, his probation officer told me that Jim was living in the same town as me (I had called her). Yes, he's been out of jail for a while. Last week when I came home, I noticed the Kool-Aid (his favorite drink) was gone from the refrigerator, the clip had been pulled out of my gun, and the closet doors were opened.

## Authors' Commentary

It is important to understand Debbie's seemingly irrational behavior—Why did she not seek help earlier? Why did she continue to help Jim despite his abuse?—for it's common in our society and typifies many survivors. According to forensic psychologist Reid Meloy (1989), Debbie behaved in a way similar to women who are battered by their spouses. Debbie and Jim had a history of violence, followed by making up through sex. Lenore Walker (1979), who has written about rape in battering relationships, specifies several phases of the battering cycle.

Walker says that sexual abuse most often takes place during the first two phases, the tension-building and acute battering phases. The sexual relationship can be quite enjoyable during phase three, the loving phase of the cycle. The positive aspects of a loving sexual relationship can act as a powerful intermittent reinforcer that allows victimization to be perpetuated and sustained. Behavioral psychologists tell us that it is very difficult to cease behavior when positive reinforcers have been applied on a random and variable schedule. Debbie permitted Jim's unpredictable and violent behavior in the hope that *this* time there would be a pleasurable aftermath.

For the battered woman, the crippling oppression does not become apparent until later in the relationship. Irrational sexual jealousy is almost universally present, even over women friends and family (Walker 1979). This would account for the self-inflicted isolation from others that Debbie reported.

Sexual intimacy is also the language of love for most battered women. Most have grown up in homes where there was some sort of violence or abuse. As Debbie stated, she was sexually abused by her stepfather as a child. An important factor is that sex becomes kinkier for the battered woman as time progresses. It takes more to stimulate the man to receive an erection and a longer time to reach orgasm. Women report being tied up and being forced to have sex with animals, other men, and objects, including food. Pain, rather than pleasure, becomes the norm (Walker 1979).

In or out of a battering situation, women who have been involved in a long-standing sexual relationship with their assaulter have a particularly difficult time with the second rape. As research has shown (Warshaw 1988), many women fail to identify themselves as victims of rape when the assaulter is an acquaintance, date, or long-term romantic partner. They question, as does society, whether he has a right to sexual access to their body. The myth of the ownership of women as property is still alive and well, as indicated by the fact that many states do not have a law protecting women from marital rape (Finkelhor and Yllo 1985). Because of this myth, which is still reflected in our laws, women often fail to protect and defend themselves adequately.

Debbie's main coping mechanism at the end was learned helplessness (Walker 1979). No matter which way she turned, she would suffer humiliation and degradation. The police officers' dismissal of her complaint is commonplace. Domestic "tiffs" are usually worked out by the parties involved, and outsiders are better off minding their own business. The hopelessness and despair felt by women trapped in an abusive relationship are very real. Society still has trouble seeing date rape as a crime.

All of these factors—her close relationship with the attacker, their previous consensual sexual relationship, and her inability to seek help and take appropriate medical steps—made Debbie appear guilty of bad judgment. She entered the legal arena with many strikes against her. Debbie eventually did feel rage about Jim's wrongdoing, however, and she believed he would be punished by those designated to help her.

Debbie was a member of a rape survivor's support group conducted by one of the authors. All of the women in the group felt that they had been tricked into accepting an unfair bargain. Many reported being misled. Debbie could not believe that the perpetrator could be deemed not dangerous by a psychiatrist and, despite his admission of guilt, could be walking around free in several weeks. Debbie also felt bitter that she had been boxed in by social appropriateness. She was sorry that she hadn't been more aggressive—not just with the rapist but also with the police and the district attorney.

Like most survivors, Debbie's fear stayed with her for a long time. Her reactions to the rape did not end with the preceding interview. Six months after the interview, she was out with friends at a crowded club. She felt herself being pushed onto the dance floor by bodies that were touching her in an aggressive way. The next thing she knew, she was screaming. She looked around to see the embarrassed reactions of her friends and others. "They could never understand," she said. But there are many women who can.

# 5

# Mercedes's Story: Attempted Rape

It was a cool December night, and my boyfriend called to see if I could go out for the evening. Since I'm only fifteen, I still have to check in with my mom to get her approval. She's a custodian at the local high school, and I usually can't reach her by telephone, so I usually just walk up there and see her. It's only a few blocks from my house.

She generally is cleaning in the cafeteria at 7 P.M., but that particular night she wasn't there. I walked around the building looking for her. While I was looking for her, I saw this guy go up and talk to a woman who was selling tickets to a play that was going on. Later, in court, I found out that he was talking to her about a lot of personal things and she got scared so she went inside the school.

After she went inside the school, the same guy came toward me and started following me down a path. He looked like he was about twenty years old and was kind of short with a stocky body. His hair was really short, kind of a like a marine haircut. Even though I was ignoring him, he started to speak to me and ask me personal questions, such as what my phone number was, how old I was, if I had any children, and if I was happy. I tried to talk with him as little as possible because his questions were really out of line and I kind of started getting scared, so I just kept walking. He even tried to kiss me four or five times, and I kept pushing him away. I told him about my boyfriend, Bob. He said, "I'll never have to see you again, and Bob will never have to find out about this." Then he wanted to know if Bob and I were happy, and he kept commenting on how nice my body looked and whether I worked out.

The next thing I knew, he must have grabbed me from behind because I was down on the ground behind the school and close to some thick bushes. I knew no one could see him there, and he said, "Say a fucking word and I'll break your fucking neck." When I started fighting and clawing his face, he said, "You bitch." I started yelling "Rape!" and by this time I was more mad than scared. He tore my shirt and was fondling my breasts, but he couldn't get my jeans down. They were really tight. I almost wore a skirt that night, but I'm so glad I didn't. He might have succeeded in raping me if I had had a skirt on. I was able to throw him off me (I guess all my practice of wrestling with friends has helped me fight). He got up and started running, and I started chasing him, still yelling "Rape!" Three guys who were helping with the play must have heard my screams because they started chasing him, too. They jumped in a car and chased him, caught him, and held him until the police came.

I was shaking and crying by this time, and a couple of girls took me to the back of the performing arts room. I must have been in shock because I really couldn't hear anything that was going on around me. Somebody found my mother and brought her in to see me. My mom got pretty hysterical because I was bleeding from my mouth (I had a cut on the side of my lip and two cuts inside my mouth).

Two policemen came, but I really don't remember what they looked like or what they even asked me. They put me in the police car and took me on a drive-by so I could identify this guy and know that he had been caught. Then they took me to the hospital, and my mom followed us in her car. We got there about 11 P.M., but the doctor didn't see me until about two or three in the morning. The doctor was really cold, and he didn't ask me any questions. He just looked at me and said, "You're fine." He didn't even examine my whole body, or he might have seen some bruises that started to show up later because of the struggle that we had had. I was glad to be told that I was fine, although I didn't really feel fine. I had never been so nervous or stunned in my whole life.

For several days after the attack, I was so hyper that I couldn't sleep or eat. I felt more angry than scared. I felt like getting a shotgun and going after him. Just to keep myself occupied at night, I would rearrange the closets and the cabinets. Pretty soon my mom couldn't find anything because I had changed things around so much. I guess it was just because I was so nervous. I couldn't concentrate in school, and since I wasn't sleeping, I took about a month off. I still can't undress for PE (physical education); it just makes me feel too weird or something, like everybody knows from looking at my body that I was attacked.

The attack happened on Friday, and I saw the district attorney on Monday. He was so nice to me and seemed to really care. He kept reassuring me that he would nail this guy one way or another. He spent a lot of time on my case, and he even went to the school where I was attacked so that we could videotape the sequence of the whole thing. I got so scared when we were taping, remembering in detail what had happened that night, but I was reassured by the district attorney that this would help my case. He talked with my psychologist on many occasions and told her he felt this was an open-and-shut case. He was so positive because the prosecution had witnesses—the woman whom he had approached before attacking me and the three guys who chased him.

There was a wonderful article in the newspaper about the three young men who helped chase and catch my attacker. They were honored at a ceremony sponsored by the sheriff's department. According to this article, the three men had heard me yelling "Rape!" and they saw that I was bleeding from my mouth. They chased my attacker, caught him, and then went to a nearby apartment complex and dialed 911.

In the same article, the incident was described as the assailant following me on the school grounds and trying to strike up a conversation with me, telling me that I was pretty. I walked away, and when I looked back, he was gone. Later he jumped out of some bushes and grabbed me. I scratched his face, and he slugged me in the mouth. As I was screaming, he tried to rape me and then ran away. The sheriff's department awarded a certificate of appreciation to the three men who had assisted in the apprehension of a dangerous and violent sex offender.

That article really made me feel good because it told the story so accurately, and I certainly thought it would help my case. Even though there was so much evidence against him, he pled not guilty, so I had to go to court. The defense attorney was a real number one asshole, and he tried to confuse me by mixing up dates and times and where I was standing when I was attacked. Then he tried to insinuate lots of things about my boyfriend, Bob, and me—like we were into drugs and having sex, so I was probably just missing Bob and flirting with my attacker. I think I held my own pretty well, but after I sat down, I cried. I cried out of frustration because I felt that the defense attorney had been unfair. The district attorney said that I had done a really excellent job and that we had nothing to worry about. In fact, he told me that he had really got on the defense attorney about harassing me and that that kind of harassment wouldn't be allowed to happen again.

After that first court date, there was an article in the newspaper that made me furious. It was so contradictory to the first article. First, the press was not supposed to use my name, but they did. Second, they twisted the information and made me look ridiculous, like I was confused, and the article made him look wonderful. The article was definitely biased in favor of my attacker. For example, in the article he said that I had set him up. He related that he was just having a friendly conversation with me when all of a sudden I gazed at him with a weird look in my eye, told him I liked to wrestle, and then slapped him and started screaming 'Rape!'." He said in the same article that he hit me because I screamed and that he took off running because he didn't know what else to do. The article described my attacker as a clean-cut ambulance corpsman. He said that he felt that I would surely alert police that the whole incident was a mistake and that I was overreacting. He was shocked and dismayed that I had decided to press charges.

His account of the assault was that I had asked him for help locating my mom. After a short walk, he said, I climbed up on a stone wall and asked if he wanted to see me jump. When I jumped, he said, he grabbed my wrist and we both fell on the ground. Then I started screaming "Rape!" and he got scared and ran. When I read that article, I just couldn't believe it. It was so unfair and came out before the second trial date. It certainly must have influenced anybody who read it. I felt like suing the newspaper. After all, I'm only fifteen, and I thought it would be illegal to put my name in the paper like that.

To make matters worse, because some of my friends saw the article, they started ignoring me. The phone calls stopped coming so frequently, and to top it all off, my boyfriend broke up with me. Here I was the victim, and everyone was treating me like I had done something wrong. My mom and I tried talking to a personal injury attorney, but he said that the case wasn't a strong one because I hadn't been hurt badly enough. We thought maybe the school should have had some liability because of the lack of security, but so far no one wants to take the case.

By the time the second court date came along, my spirits were renewed. I thought, "At last this will be over and he will be behind bars." The district attorney was still saying that this was an open-and-shut case and that he would be punished.

During my second testimony, the defense attorney was not quite as brutal, but he did try to dig into my sexual past. He kept trying to get me to admit that I had been molested when I really hadn't been. He also tried to cast doubts about my using drugs, but I have never used drugs. And then he tried to get me to talk about which boyfriends I had had sex with. I was on the stand nearly all day, and I was exhausted. Still, the district attorney said I had done an excellent job and we had nothing to worry about.

I believe it was the biggest shock and disappointment of my life when the verdict at the end of the trial was not guilty. The district attorney explained that there was not enough physical evidence, meaning that I was not hurt badly enough, to convict him for attempted rape. But worse than that, the count of assault was dropped, too. I went home angrier than I had ever been in my life. I thought the jury would put him behind bars. Instead, when the trial was over, some of the jurors went over to hug and kiss him. I guess they felt sorry for him because he cried when he was on the stand. I think he was crying because he was telling so many lies.

I couldn't understand what happened that day, so I asked my psychologist if she would talk to the district attorney. She did call him, and he told her that I had done everything right but that the jury could not find such a clean-cut, hardworking, churchgoing man guilty. He said that if the guy had looked like a scum bag, we probably would have gotten a guilty verdict.

One of the worst parts of this nightmare is that it hasn't ended for me. He doesn't live very far from me, and I've seen him in his car. He was seen in our local grocery store giving some woman a look up and down her body. That just gives me the creeps. He even

has a wife, and surely she must know. I don't think I was the first person he attacked, and I don't think I will be the last. I wonder how often he will have to do this before he gets caught and put in prison. Something tells me that since he got away with it with me, he will do it again.

I wish the district attorney had prepared me a little bit for the outcome. Not once did he give any indication that things could go the way they did. It's really not his fault that he was so positive, but I guess he's learned not to be so confident.

Right now I'm trying to convince the principal at my school to let me give an assembly on rape. I feel a very strong desire to do this so other girls can be aware and careful. About two weeks ago, I heard that one of my friends was walking to the store in broad daylight and was raped by four men. I feel I need to tell and warn people about what has happened to me and other young women.

I'm getting resistance from my principal, so I circulated a petition and have more than 450 signatures of students and teachers who would like for me to give an assembly. My psychologist called the principal, and the principal told her that our school doesn't have all-student assemblies. That's a lie because that morning we had a wrestling assembly. Why is it that the victim has so much trouble being heard? I'm not sorry I fought back, because he couldn't complete the rape. But I am furious that justice wasn't done. It makes me feel that the victim has to take justice into her own hands. I feel I will be ready next time he or anyone else tries to assault me, and I would fight to kill, since justice was not done in the courtroom.

## Authors' Commentary

Mercedes had a few strikes against her that many people fail to acknowledge. First, teenagers in our culture are looked upon with suspicion. Part of the acting-out behavior of teens involves acting out sexually, using drugs, and academic failure. This certainly is not true of all teenagers, but most parents dread their children's teen years and are highly critical of them if they act out in any manner. Part of the hypercritical judgment of teenagers is the fact that many people expect them to lie and break rules; therefore, the credibility of teens is in question.

Another strike against Mercedes was that she engaged in conversation with the attacker. Men and women often perceive what is said in that communication differently. In general, men give a more sexual reading to behavior and conversation than do women. According to Robin Warshaw (1988),

> Many men discount what a woman is saying, or reinterpret it to fit what they want to hear. They have been raised to believe that women will always resist sex to avoid the appearance of being promiscuous, will say NO when they mean YES, and will want men to dominate them and show that they are in control. Many men have been conditioned to ignore women when they say NO, even if they are pushing, fighting, kicking or crying. (p. 42)

In Mercedes's case, this ingrained philosophy may have played a part in the jury's verdict of not guilty. Justice will not be served consistently until society adopts the attitude that when a woman says no, she means it. In addition, many people cannot believe that a nice-looking man would rape a woman or that a woman would not enjoy this sexual contact.

Almost one year later, Mercedes is finally getting over the disappointment of the verdict. She also has been promised by her school counselor that she can help to lead a support group for other teens who have been physically and sexually assaulted. She has been able to turn a negative situation into a positive one in which she not only can rebuild her own self-esteem but also help others in the process.

# 6

# Katie's Story: Rape by Rank

At last my eighteenth birthday—the legal age to do many things and finally old enough to join the military. Joining the military seemed like a really good idea. It was a way to get some training, see the world, and grow up and get away from home. My decision was definite after I talked with a recruiter. He was so respectful of me—opening doors, willing to answer questions, and arranging transportation. He bent over backward to make me feel comfortable about my decision to enlist and said it was a great opportunity for women. I thought that because he was so respectful, the military would be that way, too. Unfortunately, I was dead wrong. The night before I left, I got cold feet, as I had never really been out of my hometown, much less halfway across the United States. But I just kept telling myself, "There's no turning back now, and if you do everything you're told, you'll be okay."

Before the plane had landed, other recruits were telling horror stories about what they had heard was in store for us. The stories were far more accurate than the false promises of the recruiter. We hadn't even stepped off the overloaded elbow-to-eye and armpit-to-nose bus when a deep, horrifying voice was ripping the shit out of everyone. I was terrified. I knew I was no longer my own person but belonged to the government.

As I stepped off the bus, the other recruits were getting into formation, so I followed along and did the same. As time progressed, I learned what to do and what not to do. If my drill sergeant said "Speak," I spoke; if he said "Jump," I asked how high; if he said "Get down," I got down fast. I soon learned that signing that paper and raising my right hand meant giving up myself to the man who wore the sergeant's stripes. The one sentence that sticks with me today is "Your mama ain't gonna help you now because you belong to the military." I soon learned not to ask questions about why I should do something but just to obey. The discipline engraved on me was convincing—maybe too convincing.

Basic training scared the hell out of me, and that's what it was supposed to do. I had a good attitude, did what I was told, passed basic, and was prepared mentally and physically for my future in the military.

I was sent to another base for my special school. I didn't get the exact school that I wanted or that the recruiter had promised me, but now I realize that that happens to many new recruits. The recruiters are masters at persuasion and false promises.

It was hot and humid in this hellhole where I was to learn new skills by attending class and having hands-on experience. I was in my glory. I am mechanically inclined and knew I was doing well. My sergeant would view my project, watch me work, and then move me on to the next lesson. I had eight courses to complete, and that could have been accomplished in as little as eight weeks. Instead of an eight-week course, however, my stay turned out to be six months of no school and living hell.

It all started in my fourth course. I was moving at a fast pace, but for some reason I was unable to satisfy the sergeant in charge of this course. I couldn't understand it, especially since I had helped two other classmates pass their inspections. One day I asked the sergeant what he was finding wrong with my project. He walked over to my project, looked at it, looked at me, and then looked back at the project. With a smart-ass smirk on his face, he pulled on a part of the project and said, "This isn't secure." I said, "It was before you pulled on it." And he said, "Are you questioning me?" I shut up.

Then in a calm way he said, "You know, if you scratch my back, I'll scratch yours, and maybe you'll get out of here faster than the others." I wasn't sure what he meant, and the thought crossed my mind that maybe he meant a sexual gesture, but I just couldn't and didn't want to believe that. You see, fraternalization is a serious offense in the military, and I trusted that as my superior, he wouldn't break such a critical rule.

It was time for cleanup, and the sergeant assigned everyone else to cleanup duty on the grounds. He sent me to the ladies' room to clean it. As I opened the door and looked around, I realized that this bathroom was not even in use. It was old, and there were boards over the toilets and cobwebs hanging all over. As I turned around and was walking toward the door, my sergeant walked in with a big shit-eating grin on his face and said, "Lock the door." I asked why, and he said, "If you ever want to get out of here, lock the door."

I was sure now about his plan. I walked over to the door and locked it like I was ordered to do, with my heart sinking to the pit of my stomach. He walked over and stared me in the face and said, "Unbutton your pants. You want me as bad as I want you. Let's just have some fun and a really good fuck, and you'll never have to see me again. I'll get you out of here for sure and pass you on your project today."

I begged him not to do this to me and wouldn't undo my pants. He got aggressive and shoved me against the wall and ripped my pants open. All the time he kept saying, "Don't scream or make a noise because who do you think they'll believe—a little private or an experienced sergeant?"

Then he started sticking his tongue in and out and tried to French-kiss me. I held my teeth closed tight. He started talking dirty to me and said he knew I wanted his cock so bad, deep inside of me, and that he could give it to me better than anyone. He kept holding his dick and wanted me to suck on it, but I kept turning my head and closing my teeth tight. He backed me up against a wall and held my neck with his hands and shoved his cock between my legs. I was numb, and I didn't feel him penetrate. (Later hospital reports confirmed penetration.)

I pushed him away from me, saying, "I don't want to have a black baby," and he replied that he never left any evidence. Then he came into his own hand and said, "See, you're not going to be pregnant."

Then he said, "Just walk out there calm and act like nothing happened or else I'll tell them I was disciplining you and you cried rape." He told me to join the others, and I started picking up cigarette butts. I felt numb, like none of this had really happened. Then a few hours later, he was leading a formation, and he kept looking at me. I felt so humiliated that I kept looking at the ground. When I went back to the barracks, everyone was chatting and getting ready to go to lunch. I felt sick and just kept walking around trying to figure out what to do.

My squad leader came by, and I told her in confidence what had happened. I wanted her opinion about what I should do. It felt good to tell someone, but I didn't know she would tell someone else. Then a few hours later, I was sitting in my barracks, and all of a sudden someone said, "Man on board—attention." That means someone is entering the premises. I was scared to death that it was him, my sergeant. I was relieved that it wasn't him but the commanding officer.

My relief soon turned to humiliation and embarrassment, as I was questioned by the commanding officer with a group of military police around me. It was agony to be interrogated about a crime I didn't commit. At first I lied and told them that a black man had come out of the woods, held a knife to my throat, and raped me in a little shed by the edge of the woods. I was convinced that they would not believe me if I told the truth. I said I had never seen the man before, as I was scared of my attacker. I knew right away that they didn't believe me because they said that 90 percent of the time in the military women cry rape and it's not true.

The military cover-up was unbelievable. They took me to a hospital many miles away, made me dress in civilian clothes, drove me in an unmarked car, and wouldn't let me call my mother. They ran all the medical tests and didn't give me any information about their findings. When I was allowed to tell my mom about the rape, she was mad that I hadn't put up more of a physical fight. You see, everyone has always seen me as having a lot of spunk and grit and being very strong. Therefore, I told her the stranger-knife story, knowing that she would really be angry with me if there was no weapon involved.

My story got more and more complicated, and I knew I was in deep shit when they investigated the shed that I said he had raped me in and they found bloodstains there. Since I had no puncture wounds, I became highly nervous about my story. Later it was discovered that a maintenance man had cut himself and left bloodstains. My story was inconsistent, and I began to get more and more uneasy with the lies. I cracked and told the truth after being awakened in the middle of the night at 2 or 3 A.M. by their interrogation. When I finally told the truth, they didn't believe me. They suggested that my sergeant and I must have been having sex and that I discovered I was pregnant and yelled rape.

Rumors began spreading around the base, and lots of people were asking me what happened. I felt so exposed and on display. In a public meeting, everyone was instructed not to ask me about the rape, and if anyone was heard talking about it, they would be disciplined. That order didn't stop the looks I got or the whispers.

I was told very little about the investigation but was reassured that the sergeant had been shipped off the base and I wouldn't have to see him again. I was sent home for two weeks, and when I told my mom the truth, she was furious and yelled at me for two reasons. She was mad that I had lied, and she was angry about the rape itself. She didn't really believe it was a traumatic assault, and I felt more ashamed than ever. It was a very uncomfortable two weeks at home because my mom blamed me for what had happened. I was sent back to the same base, but I wasn't allowed to finish school. Instead, I was given every shitty detail there was and spent the next six months pulling weeds in the hot sun. They treated me like dirt. Whenever I asked about the investigation, I was told, "We know how to handle it."

They were preparing me for trial because I was told he wasn't pleading guilty. My attorney kept grilling me about details, trying to confuse me because he said that's what the defense attorney would do. Truthfully, I'm not even sure my own attorney even believed me. Each time I had to meet with him, I was upset for days. The one piece of convincing evidence on my behalf was that the medical exam revealed that some of his pubic hairs were caught in the buttons of my pants. There also was evidence of forced penetration, as I hadn't had any sexual contact for months previously.

No one bothered to tell me that the case was closed until I asked after several weeks of hearing nothing. They told me that he kept changing his story and failed the lie detector test three times, so they discharged him from military service. It was rumored that he had a wife and children and that I was not the first person he had raped, but I was the only one who had had any evidence. I still don't know what really happened to him or where he is. He knows my name, and I have this fear that he might look me up and kill me because I told. After all, maybe I ruined his career.

After the case was closed, I was relieved to be sent to another base and to start school again. I felt that I would have a fresh start with no rumors. I was wrong again. You see, your military records follow you everywhere. On my next base assignment, I injured my leg. When my sergeant asked me to march, I explained my leg injury. He said, "Okay, private, but I've read your file, and don't think you're going to pull the same stunt on me that you did on your last sergeant." Again I felt unjustly judged and that I had this black mark against me for having been raped.

If I had it all to do over again, I probably wouldn't tell. The punishment, shame, and humiliation I felt in the months afterward were worse than the rape itself. I don't even know if telling made a difference. He may be out of the military, but maybe he's still a rapist or abusive to women in some way.

Maybe I would be glad I told if it had happened in the civilian world because I think I would have been more informed. There is such secrecy and cover-up in the military because of the good old boy syndrome, sort of like "I'll take care of you so this doesn't leak to the press and give the military a bad rap." I don't really think they value or want women in the military. I refused to be a sex object, but that was what I was expected to be. All that respect the recruiter gave me was a sham. I wish he had told me the way it really is—that rank has its privileges even to the point of rape.

## Authors' Commentary

The military can be fertile ground for female victimization. Rape has a long history in the military. It was frowned upon by the more civilized kings and generals but remained a hallmark of success in battle. In medieval times, opportunities to rape and loot were among the few "advantages" open to common foot soldiers, who were paid irregularly (Brownmiller 1975).

Through the ages, triumph over women by rape became a way to measure victory—part of a soldier's proof of masculinity and success, a tangible reward for services rendered (Brownmiller 1975).

The movie *Casualties of War* presents a case of rape and assault during the Vietnam War. It indicates that some of the same military attitudes of power and justification of female victimization still exist today. In this movie, a platoon captures a young Vietnamese woman and several men in the platoon rape and physically abuse her. Some of the men in the platoon justify their actions by saying that death may be imminent and they should enjoy sexual release even if it means the subjugation of a woman. Another attitude portrayed in this movie is that all Vietnamese are enemies and they should be punished for the loss of American lives. Some of the men in this platoon are intimidated by their superior into following orders to rape and abuse female captives. They go against their own moral code to obey authority and to be considered one of the boys.

Katie's story is an example of intimidation by someone in authority. In basic training, the military brainwashes recruits that they must obey. The concept of submissiveness is encouraged, and assertiveness is not allowed. Authority is idealized. Through the years, women have been viewed as objects to play with and have fun with while military men are on leave or in port. Some men are angry that women have been allowed and encouraged to join the military. Others feel as though women are not as competent as men, and some are threatened by women's competence.

Katie speaks of military cover-ups, which are apparent in the movie *Casualties of War*. One soldier tells his commanding officer about what happened with the Vietnamese woman, but the officer encourages him to keep quiet and insinuates that these types of things happen all the time. He tells the soldier that turning in his buddies would be a betrayal of them, since they have fought together to save each other's lives. Eventually in this movie, the chaplain takes action, and justice is finally served. Although military cover-ups regarding rape no doubt still occur, one encouraging factor is that today some perpetrators of rape who are in the military have been prosecuted both in public trials and in military trials. The authors believe that justice would be enhanced if all rapists faced public scrutiny as well as military prosecution.

Katie's story also exemplifies the fact that someone in a subservient position often is not believed when challenging or accusing a person in authority. She thought she had to lie to substantiate her victimization. Her own mother did not want to believe that a person in authority could be a rapist, so she chose to blame her daughter, adding to Katie's sense of shame and humiliation.

Survivors like Katie give us hope for the future. Today she is out of the military, has a good job, and is going to college. When asked what she thinks about young women going into the military, she says, "They need to be more realistically and intelligently informed. They also need to be told about sexual harassment, what to do about it, and how to see the signs of harassment, and they need to realize that military obedience doesn't ever mean sacrificing your body."

# 7

# Red's Story: A Parable of Rape

My real name is Elizabeth, but everyone has always called me "Red," that being my favorite color to wear. I'm young and single and live with my mother in a house on the edge of town.

Well, early one morning, my mother said, "Red, I want you to take this homemade loaf of bread and pot of chicken soup to your grandmother. She's sick, and this will really help her feel better."

I was quite excited to venture out from my home. I wasn't afraid; in fact, the outside world seemed to offer such beauty and pleasure. I've always been the inquisitive type; I like to find out about things, but I don't get the chance often. I put on my new red velvet coat that Grandmother had made me, but before I walked out the door—picnic basket packed with goodies in hand—my mother sat me down and talked to me seriously.

"Red," she said, "I want you to listen very carefully to me. Grandmother lives way across town on the edge of the woods. I want you to hurry, dear, and don't go off the main road. Don't daydream and dawdle like you sometimes do. Make sure you don't forget your manners. Nice girls always say good morning, please, and thank you. Grandmother is quite old and gets tired easily, so have a nice visit but come straight home and be careful."

I promised I would do as she said, but I wasn't worried because I knew the road well. Waving good-bye to Mom, I pulled the hood of my coat down over my head and set forth on my journey.

On the road to Grandmother's house, everything was so alive and interesting. About halfway to Grandmother's, however, I started feeling a little lonely. There were people passing along the road, but they were strangers and nobody stopped to talk to me. That's when I met Harry.

He came up to me and was very friendly. He had a really big smile. He seemed to know me and said, "Good morning, Red." I guess we'd met before, but I didn't know too much about him. I was polite (as mother had trained me) when I answered, "Good morning, Harry." He was very large, kind of old, and really hairy (must be how he got his name). He didn't seem at all frightening and was nice enough. So we had this conversation.

He asked me where I was headed, and I told him to Grandmother's. I said, "She's sick in bed, you know." He seemed really interested in me and looked right into my eyes. He was also very interested in Grandmother, and I thought that was nice. He inquired about what I had in my basket, and I told him. He asked me where she lived, and I willingly gave him the exact directions to her house. I guess I thought he might go there sometime and wish her a speedy recovery.

Harry walked along with me for a while. Just having him there to talk to made the trip so much more interesting. He pointed out all the beautiful flowers along the road and said, "For goodness sake. Why don't you relax a bit and look at the world and see how lovely it is? Listen to the birds singing; feel the sunshine on your face. Don't be so solemn and well behaved as if you were going to school or work." I must admit that together everything seemed gay and magical. I no longer felt the slightest bit lonely as we ventured farther and farther from the main road.

Sunlight danced through the trees; butterflies scattered among the ferns. I suddenly got the idea that Grandmother would appreciate a bunch of flowers, so I said good-bye to Harry and wandered off among the trees to pick the prettiest ones. I guess it took some time. I became so engrossed in finding the most beautiful flowers, and I was enjoying myself so much.

Sometime later, I remembered the promise I'd made to Mother. I found my way back to the main road and walked straight to Grandmother's house.

When I got to the door, something didn't seem quite right. I started to feel frightened when I found the door open. I couldn't understand why I was so upset, so I dismissed my thoughts of danger. After all, what was there to fear? I proceeded inside, cautiously at first.

I called for Grandmother, but there was no answer. I went quietly into the bedroom and saw her lying in bed, a shawl drawn over her face. She looked very strange, but I couldn't figure out why. I thought, "She's old and been sick." I couldn't help but stare. I noticed her hairy ears and hands, her shiny eyes, and her big sharp teeth. When I commented on the strangeness I observed, Grandmother invited me to join her in bed. "Come lie beside me, my dear," she said. I was curious to find out more—excited and yet sensing danger—but I complied.

Once in bed, I had this sinking feeling that I was stuck in a dreadful circumstance from which I could not escape. When Grandmother threw off her shawl and revealed herself to be Harry, I was frozen with fear. How could I have been tricked so? What had happened to dear Grandmother? Harry engulfed me with his violent passion. I remained passive as he devoured and invaded my very flesh inch by inch. I could not scream; I could not fight. He was such an animal, overpowering me with his brute strength. I thought I was dying.

Fortunately, passing by Grandmother's house was a hunter who heard Harry's animal sounds after he had done his violent act. By this time, I was forever gone from the world in a place so dark I thought I would never live again. The hunter thought something was strange and stopped in. He entered on a scene of total destruction and annihilation. But Harry, content at last after his overpowering rape, was caught off guard. The hunter immediately freed me from the clutches of Harry, who fled from the house into the woods. "He'll never bother you again," the kind hunter said.

"You rescued me," I said. "I am so thankful to you." I was so frightened. That was the darkest moment of my life. I thought I would be forever gone. "But where's Grandmother?" I asked.

A closet door opened and out stepped Grandmother, alive but hardly able to breathe from fright and exhaustion. She, too, had been a victim of Harry's deception, evil, and unspeakable wrongdoing. We thanked the hunter with all our hearts. Grandmother and I were so glad to be alive that we hugged each other and shook the hunter's hand over and over again.

Since that time, I've begun to feel healthier and stronger, it took us some time to clean up the mess that Harry had made in our lives. I myself have learned a lot from the incident with Harry. I have vowed never to take risky journeys out in the world. I used to forget my duties and stray off into exciting but dangerous areas. I also feel as though I let my mother down for not heeding her warnings and staying on the safe path, remaining cautious and alert for all signs of danger. But then Harry seemed so nice, and Mother has always told me to be polite. Sometimes it's hard to know when to be polite and whom to trust—especially since I'm so young and don't get out much.

I've also worried about how I dress. If I go out of the house, I wear the drabbest colors. I feel guilty that my red velvet coat could have attracted Harry's unwanted attention.

I am so thankful that the hunter came along and rescued me from Harry's clutches. If he hadn't protected me, I would be gone forever, and so would grandmother. They haven't been able to find Harry, and sometimes I wonder where he is. I also wonder why the hunter didn't use his gun to kill him. But I'm alive, and that's what matters.

Mother has told me that there are men out there in the world who prey on young single girls who are alone. These men trick us and seduce us by being nice and friendly. But they are really animals. I should have kept my promise to Mother, so I guess it was my fault. I am comforted, though, that at least I minded my manners and through the whole ordeal always said good morning, please, and thank you.

## Authors' Commentary

The preceding is, of course, an adaptation of the classic fairy tale *Little Red Riding Hood*. According to Bruno Bettleheim (1976), the story exists in several versions. The preceding is a combination of the most popular versions.

The first rendering of this fairy tale was written by French writer Charles Perrault in 1697. It was intended to provide a cautionary moral and ends with the wolf being victorious. This version is quite explicit, as the girl undresses and joins the wolf in bed as he tells her that his strong arms are for embracing her better. Little Red

Riding Hood makes no move to escape or fight back, leaving the reader to conclude that she is either stupid or wants to be seduced.

In the Brothers Grimm version of 1812 (Bettleheim 1976), "Little Red Cap" and the grandmother are reborn (cut from the wolf's stomach), and the wolf is given a well-deserved punishment. Instead of the fallen woman of the Perrault version, Red is a naive and innocent girl, and therefore is a more suitable figure to identify with. She is torn between her desires for pleasure and the warnings of adults.

Regardless of which version one reads, *Little Red Riding Hood* has much in common with the stories of the rape survivors that appear earlier in this book. Susan Brownmiller (1975) states that women are trained to be rape victims. Children who have read and been read this "innocent" fairy tale for centuries are exposed to words of caution that seep into their subconscious and indoctrinate them in a victim mentality.

A young girl leaves the safety of her parents' home and ventures into the outside world with the warning not to stray from the well-known road. Despite this warning, she goes out willingly to do an altruistic and adventuresome act. She overlooks the dangerous aspects of her choices (as Lydia and Debbie did) to be a liberated female. But the outcome is hardly good; she is tricked and betrayed. The moral is clear: it is better to stick to the safe path. In other words, women should stay in their place, or harm will befall them. Red Riding Hood is lucky because a friendly man rescues her from certain disaster. In fairy tales, it takes a man to do the fighting. Jack in the Beanstalk can kill the giant, but Little Red Riding Hood, Sleeping Beauty, and Cinderella are passive and immobile until rescued by men. Thus, the second moral is that women are helpless without men. They cannot ensure their own survival.

There are other commonalities between Red and the rape survivors. In both the parable and the survivors' stories, the women put considerable emphasis on proper feminine behavior (being polite and not creating a scene). In Red's appraisal of her actions after being attacked by the wolf, she is pleased with herself in this regard. Many survivors feel acutely embarrassed and ashamed if they do create a scene by telling or otherwise becoming hysterical in front of others. Also like Red, many survivors numb their feelings during the rape, a coping mechanism women have learned through centuries of feeling powerless while being overwhelmed physically. And finally like Red, many survivors scrutinize their own behavior to learn what they did wrong to cause the rape to occur. One cannot help but feel frustrated with Red's lack of discretion in telling the wolf the exact location of where she's going. This naive trust makes her look foolish and blameworthy and adds to her own and others' confusion over who was really at fault. Blaming oneself could be called the hallmark symptom of the survivor. No doubt fairy tales such as *Little Red Riding Hood* help cement the logic instilled by a society that continues to put women in a "one-down" position and keep them there by way of guilt and fear.

# PART THREE

# The Second Rapists

# 8

# The Police

**M**ost of us have been raised with a media image of the investigators of crime as strong, protective men with an unflinching will to track down their suspect and see him behind bars. Magnum, Hunter, and Dirty Harry devote their entire day, it would seem, to this relentless pursuit. In addition, they offer emotional solace to the rape survivor. They even go so far as to offer her their apartment for respite from the stalker and provide a twenty-four-hour bodyguard service.

Unfortunately, such an image could not be further from the truth. As one detective stated, "By the time one of our guys finishes his day at the local bar, he often can't even remember a victim's name or the circumstances of her case." The fact is that our public safety servants are overworked and have neither the time nor the inclination to focus all their energy on one suspect or the well-being of one survivor. "Victims seem to think that we should drop what we're doing and attend to their case and their needs," the detective said. "This is very frustrating at times."

Our naive attitudes toward the police begin with the assumption that all police personnel are equally knowledgeable about and experienced with rape. When one detective was asked whether a rape survivor's credibility would be judged initially by her attractiveness, he replied, "It depends on whether you talk to a guy who's just come out of the academy, a patrolman, or a detective. There's a lot of variability." Unfortunately for many rape survivors, a call to 911 can have discouraging results. As another detective stated, "Maybe

50 to 70 percent of initial responses are by rookies with little to no exposure to rape complaints outside of the classroom." This fact alone has far-reaching ramifications when we consider that this person has the power to determine the entire direction of a case.

A survivor such as Debbie is not only hysterical and in a state of shock during the first police encounter but also is acutely sensitive to the attitudes she perceives in this person. A thoughtless innuendo can discourage the survivor in the first few minutes and hours following a rape. This time period is critical, and it is unfortunate that a sex crime investigator may not arrive to interview the woman until twelve to forty-eight hours later. By this time, as in Debbie's case, not only has the physical evidence been destroyed, but the woman's self-esteem has been destroyed as well. It is no wonder that the survivor, already embarrassed and humiliated by her assault, experiences a second rape.

It is ironic that a public safety servant, possibly with little or no experience with rape survivors, has all the power and responsibility of a judge and jury in assessing the legitimacy of a complaint. As one of the detectives we interviewed admitted, the officer may have attitudes about rape that influence his or her assessment of a case as founded or unfounded. Unlike a judge, however, the first-contact police officer will never be open to attack by a disagreeing public. Unlike jurors, he or she cannot be polled. He or she is allowed to abandon or downgrade a case silently and invisibly. Unlike the rapist, the police officer is above the law.

It was clear above all else that the police officers we interviewed wished to be thought of as objective and reliable assessors of the facts. It really did not matter, they said, if they personally believed the woman. The main question was would their boss, the district attorney, want to prosecute. To illustrate, one police detective recounted the story of a case she had recently investigated:

> A woman had gone to her employer's house to play cards. She got drunk and passed out. Upon regaining consciousness, the woman discovered she had had intercourse but didn't remember giving her consent. A woman like this who's been drinking or taking drugs would not make a credible witness. I didn't encourage her to prosecute. She may have been violated, but the district attorney wouldn't have liked this case.

Assessing a credible witness means that the police investigator must listen to determine whether the victim can articulate what happened to her before, during, and after the assault. The account must be coherent and in chronological order. "If there are contradictions and inconsistencies in her story, the defense attorney will rip her apart on the stand," the police detective stated. If alcohol or drugs were part of the crime, the woman is immediately suspect, even if her story is without loopholes. We are reminded of the gang-rape survivor in the movie *The Accused* whose hospital exam showed evidence of alcohol and marijuana in her bloodstream. Although she had obvious physical injuries from the sexual assaults and a coherent story, the information about drugs and alcohol cast doubt on her story. One detective told us,

> A weak witness is one who is not able to make a presentation in front of the court. The likely response of juries is to hold the victim responsible for an assault if she has been drinking—period. If a victim has this factor in her case and all the other evidence is good, it will be plea-bargained. In other words, it will be seen as a contributory factor and can be used to reduce the suspect's charges. Juries believe that drinking or drugs reflect on a woman's character, and she becomes the kind of person who might cause this to happen.

It is obvious that the police screen cases not so much based on objective and reliable facts but on a system that caters to the archaic myth that only certain women get raped.

The investigator also must intrude on the most private and personal details of the survivor's life. One detective said,

> We are interested in knowing of her nefarious activities because the idea of the defense is to cast doubt on the victims, and they may go to any extreme. We need to know her background as far as other contacts with law enforcement—that is, does she have a record? If a woman claiming rape has been arrested for soliciting or is a known prostitute, her charges may have merit, but they will be unfounded.

Other circumstances along the lines of prostitution also require exploration by the police:

> A victim's provocative dress will definitely be used against her. A jury is going to have a hard time with the bar scene. The main thing is

can you convince twelve people that what happened is wrong? If we think that the state won't win, then we don't file.

The police perpetrate a second rape by making a woman's character and morals an issue. They reinforce the cycle of victim blaming that makes rape the most underreported crime. This will continue to be true until rapes are investigated like any other violent crime.

Certain biographical data also are influential. A woman over age seventy and a child under age ten are perceived as more vulnerable due to their age. A married traditional homemaker is more believable than a single, sexually active woman. A teacher or social worker is more convincing as a victim than a bartender.

Finally, a woman is much more believable if her attacker is a stranger. In New York, for example, researchers studying police files found that 24 percent of rape complaints in nonstranger cases were judged by the police to be without merit, compared to 5 percent in stranger cases (Estrich 1987). In response to the question "What kind of woman gets raped?" one detective replied,

> Women never ask to be raped, but there is a certain type of woman who is culpable, apathetic, and ignorant. We call her HUA for "head up her ass." She's unable to sever former destructive relationships, and she may have a propensity to being victimized. She likes to get attention. She needs to know that somebody cares.

We asked a detective what factors determine whether he will press for the prosecution of a date rape. He replied, "I first of all would like to know if there was anything she did to help it along either covertly or overtly. I would want to know if she was just acting naturally—that is, were there honorable and noble reasons for her behavior?"

What would be a dishonorable reason? He replied,

> If she worked such and such boulevard (was a prostitute), I would also want to know how she felt about the suspect. Maybe she's really falling for this guy and has some doubts in her mind. I would want to know if she still loved him and was just upset over the relationship.

A female police investigator noted, "I get frustrated with the women. They've usually made bad decisions in life. In two years, I haven't seen a legitimate rape yet. Most of what I see is prostitutes." Like Little Red Riding Hood, women should know better.

Blame comes prominently into play in acquaintance or date rape. Prior relationships are usually considered as private disputes that should be settled outside the public prosecution system. Judging from the responses of the police interviewees, even detectives are lacking in the awareness and experience necessary to investigate these types of cases. There are stranger rapes and prostitute rapes, with a big black hole in the middle that nobody in the system wants to address.

Police have adopted the "victim-precipitated" concept to make date rape analogous to a nonstranger barroom brawl in which both parties claim that the other one started it (Estrich 1987). These two situations are, of course, not at all analogous, since a male-female dispute is not one of equal power and strength. Nevertheless, if there is any indication that the woman may have led the man on, the survivor is to blame. If a woman acts in a way that could be considered as an invitation to sexual relations—for instance, she agreed to have drinks with the man, accepted or offered him a ride, or left with him after a party—the judgment is that she should have known better. Debbie was justified when she expressed her fear of being judged culpable because her first encounter with her attacker was at a bar.

Victim-precipitated rapes are easy to find. Poor judgment on the part of the survivor is a convenient rationale having everything to do with our cultural myths and nothing to do with the fact that a crime has been committed. One police officer summed this up by saying, "These women seem to be overtrusting. They really lack caution. Well over 60 percent are preventable assaults. They start at the bar, and then she accepts a ride home. Rape happens to women who make bad decisions in life in general."

Apparently, the police merely mirror the attitudes of society. In their landmark study of jury trials, Kalven and Seisel found that juries tend to be prejudiced against the prosecution in rape cases (Estrich 1987). They will go to great lengths to be lenient with defendants if there is any suggestion of contributory behavior on the part of the survivor, including hitchhiking, dating, and talking with men at parties.

Another factor that is critical to police assessment of the woman is the level of resistance displayed by her. Despite laws that have attempted to make more lenient interpretations of "force," old attitudes about resistance remain. "No longer does a victim have to use force," one detective stated, "but she must communicate that she was not willing to go along with the sexual acts." When asked to give examples of how she could demonstrate fear for her safety, the detective mentioned squirming, struggling, and screaming.

All the interviewees affirmed that the victim must attempt to convince him that she means no in an assertive manner. "In the end, it's still her word against his," one said.

Despite the fact that force is no longer required to prove that a rape has occurred, physical injuries make a case much stronger. Lydia's nose was broken, her pubic hairs were burned, and her body was covered with graffiti. Debbie's physical injuries were not as obvious and thus were largely ignored.

Screaming, struggling, and squirming—unless witnessed by a third party willing to get involved—can be claimed by any survivor. These acts, as well as an assertive no, may have little weight in convincing the members of a jury, who have well-entrenched prejudices about how resistance must be displayed. Many people still believe the notion of "death before dishonor." In other words, only a woman willing to risk her life will be believed.

No other violent crime requires any level of victim resistance as an element of the offense. In California, similar offenses of forcible sodomy and oral copulation do not require victim resistance. In robbery, victims are not expected to fight back. In fact, law enforcement agencies recommend that victims surrender their property without a struggle.

Resistance to rape can take many forms. Bart and O'Brien (1986) state that women who fight their attackers are no more likely to be injured than those who do not struggle. However, resistance to assault can take many forms. Warshaw (1988) recommends that a woman assess the situation, her attacker's vulnerability, and her own resources to determine the best tactic. Resistance to assault does not always result in provable bruises or cuts. Feigning that she's passed out (as Lydia did) or telling the assaulter she has a venereal disease or has her period *may* be just as effective in stopping a rape. These tactics are not always successful because Lydia had her period, and the rapist knew it and still persisted.

The assessment of fear for her safety is even more troublesome when the survivor knows her attacker. The assumption held by much of society is that a woman would be less fearful if she knew the person and that, if she really wanted to, she could reason with him. This is totally inaccurate, as borne out by recent studies. Betrayal by someone known may be just as terrifying as random violence (Warshaw 1988). Knowing your attacker is no guarantee of better treatment. In fact, in cases of robbery and assault, studies find a greater likelihood of physical injury from attacks by nonstrangers than by strangers (Estrich 1987). Unfortunately, jurors are often biased by the archaic notion of "claim of right." This notion is based on the belief that if a woman has consented to sex in the past, the man has a continuing right to sexual satisfaction. Medieval property rights pertaining to the entitlement of usage at any time and place are still alive and well. This is particularly true in cases of spousal rape. The closer the relationship between victim and rapist, the more force must be exhibited.

It appears obvious that despite the removal of the resistance standard, not much has changed in the police assessment of a victim's fear for her safety. Police still look for weapons, scratches, bruises, and the elusive witness that can make the case go forward. Police detectives confirmed that they were still handling the assessment of this factor in the same way they did before force was stricken from the law. Believing that assertive behavior alone will do the job is misleading. Police who betray the woman by having her believe this are committing a second rape.

Survivors are extremely vulnerable following the rape. They may be justifiably terrified because the rapist knows where they live. One police detective advised the following:

> If he has no prior record for a violent crime, we can't go after him and lock him up just because a victim is afraid. A suspect is still innocent. I would advise a victim not to go out alone—not to do anything alone. I would teach a victim to secure her environment and be aware of her surroundings. She needs to share her experience with others and learn to love herself again.

The concept of police protection as conveyed by the media is erroneous to the point of being ludicrous. Another detective said, "The best bet for protection of the victim is a crisis center or safe house. The average victim has no idea of what police protection is. We have no extra patrol, but it sounds good. They're on their own really."

A police detective in another city noted, "We can't really offer any physical protection to rape victims. We can request an extra patrol, which means that a police officer might drive by the victim's house or apartment a little more frequently."

All the detectives interviewed suggested that the woman obtain a restraining order, but they view these orders with some skepticism. One said, "A restraining order is only good if the suspect is caught at the scene. If they're out on their own recognizance, they're not supposed to have contact with the victim or her family."

Another noted, "It's not cost-effective for us to have people be bodyguards. If she needs help, she should consult public service books on where the victim can get help—like a battered women's shelter. I wouldn't count on a patrol car or a restraining order."

It is ironic that a woman's fear for her well-being is necessary for a conviction of rape, yet there are few if any options available to protect her from the object of her fear—least of all the police. Most of the detectives interviewed said they rely on women's resource centers or rape crisis networks for the protection and education of survivors. But there is nothing these organizations can do to make an arrest.

The public would like to believe that rapists are made a top priority by the police, but here again the police depend on the woman's own resourcefulness and capacity to remember helpful details. As one police investigator stated, "We do our best to pick the guy up, but a lot depends on how good her description of him is. Many rape victims think that once they've given a brief description of the suspect, it's all up to us."

The attacker's description is vitally important, but many women may be so terrified during the attack that they close their eyes. There is also a tendency to block out painful events. If the attack is at night, all the lights may be off. In the daytime, many assailants use a disguise. One detective said,

> I try to build a solid alliance with her to make a good case. I need us to work as a team. We need to put together a composite picture of him with a good recollection of what kind of chin he has and so on.

She may be losing her memory, and I need to force her to relive the crime so that we have a case.

When a woman is fighting for her life, she needs to take notice of any helpful identifiers, or the police may have difficulty making an arrest based on a positive identification. The intrusion, although sometimes necessary, often feels like a second rape.

The most successful apprehension of a suspect for arrest may occur when the survivor plays detective. Note that both Lydia and Debbie were instrumental in locating their attackers. It is common for survivors to return to the scene of the crime time and again— sometimes with a friend—in hopes of catching a glimpse of the offender. Their tenacity and willingness to expose themselves to this danger is worthy of Dirty Harry. When questioned why the police don't do more to locate a suspect, one officer answered, "We just don't have the mechanisms to keep up with the growth of complaints. Our people are overwhelmed. We go from one call to the next, without a stop in between. There's no time to do any more than we're already doing."

Our interviewees also stressed the timeliness of reporting a crime. One said, "There's no excuse for not reporting immediately any longer. She can always report it to a hot line now." This attitude fails to take into account the myriad reasons a survivor may have for a delay.

First and foremost, women are in shock and have trouble making decisions. This is part of the crisis phase of the trauma syndrome. As has been well documented, women also have trouble admitting to themselves that they were raped. Some women, because of the community in which they live, have trouble locating resources. Lack of education about where to turn and what to do to verify the assault also are problems. The media may contribute to these problems by instilling a fear of revictimization in women. We often see stories of crime victims who come forward and then are revictimized. Finally, the criminal justice system's lack of understanding of rape may cause a victim to delay reporting the crime.

Our interviewees emphasized the importance of corroborative evidence in rape cases, but such evidence often is difficult to find. There usually are no witnesses to a rape. In addition, a medical examination may establish the fact that penetration occurred, but that proves only that the woman engaged in intercourse. Both tissue damage and semen may need to be present to determine that the intercourse was forced and to aid in identification of the perpetrator.

Although credibility, culpability, fear for the woman's safety, timeliness of reporting, and corroborative evidence are important in a rape case, no element affects the direction of the case so much as the attitude of the individual assigned to investigate the crime. Our interviews of both male and female investigators revealed a general repugnance of rape cases. One man said,

> I hate rape cases because I get involved with the victim. She doesn't know the system, and I have to walk her from A to Z. I hate the victims' ignorance. And they cling. I may encourage them to call only because they have no one else to support them. There's lots of pressure and lots of responsibility on me.

A female detective said, "I don't play the sympathy game well. I leave that to the male officers. They play the game better. We can't even polygraph the victim anymore, so we don't know if she is being truthful. That's the reality of the situation."

In response to the question of what particular group of women need more information about rape, the same detective said,

> I'm angry about the indecision of women. Give information to women at the welfare department, the mental health offices, and the military posts. The women say, "I didn't know what to do. My husband wasn't home, or my best friend and I couldn't find out what to do." These women are very dependent. These are the kind of rapes that are reported.

We pressed the detectives for solutions that would make their jobs easier. Some openly admitted to bias in the system in which they work. One said,

> I believe the pendulum of justice will ultimately swing back the other way. When I first started working in the system in 1967, we were a little right of center. Now we're moving back to the center. But all parts are not moving at the same speed at the same time. We've had a population explosion, and we operate with a lot of constraints. Law enforcement is just one part of the body. Right now I do my best job

by staying concerned with the admissibility and reliability of evidence so that I'll have my ducks lined up to sell the district attorney on my project.

Another added,

There are some flaws in our system. I'm opposed to having a generalist in trauma cases. Some area detectives work on a rotation system, with no expertise in any area.

We need to have a crisis team meeting with the police involved at least bimonthly. The victim, hot line workers, and the police need to meet within the first forty-eight hours. There still needs to be more focus on the victim. The police need more education on victimology and more updated classes.

In general, those interviewed said that the police needed to be more aware of the survivor's state of mind. They recognize that they get hardened and lose their empathy for victims. Despite legal changes that give victims more rights, some detectives noted that things don't always happen the way the law intended. There are too many cases, and women still don't know their options.

It was obvious from our interviews that police personnel use the same defenses as the general public to distance themselves from rape. If women believe that only certain kinds of women get raped, they can feel less vulnerable. If men can place part of the blame on the survivor, they can partially deny that their own gender could do something so abhorrent.

When a woman reports a rape, she's taking an unknown path. On the one hand, she may be assigned a special police investigator who is sensitive to her and expends much energy on her behalf. The investigator's personality, attitudes, and training may encourage the woman and enhance her self-esteem. On the other hand, insensitive and overworked police personnel may be part of the second rape.

# 9

# Medical Personnel

The initial physical and emotional response to the aftermath of rape has been termed the acute phase of the rape trauma syndrome. This cluster of symptoms has been documented in the literature based on the responses of many survivors (Burgess and Holmstrom 1979). The immediate impact of the incident leaves the survivor with intense feelings of shock and disbelief. She also may fear for her life even though her assailant has left the scene. Survivors report feelings of humiliation, degradation, shame, and embarrassment in conjunction with the prevailing feeling of fear. The tendency is for women to want to crawl off and hide after the rape. Linda, a twenty-six-year-old survivor of a date rape at gunpoint, said, "After he left, I stayed alone huddled in the corner of my bedroom with a blanket over me. I felt paralyzed. I couldn't move. I was afraid he'd come after me again. I must have stayed this way for two days. I lost track of time."

Many survivors also report physical symptoms following the rape that make it difficult to seek medical attention. The sexual violence can result in general soreness or may be focused on the specific area that was targeted for attack, such as vaginal or anal pain, or, in the case of oral sex, irritation to the mouth or throat. It no doubt takes great strength and courage for these women to subject themselves to the further physical invasion and scrutiny of a medical examination.

Despite the victim's emotional and physical state, she must get medical documentation of her injuries immediately for corroborative evidence to be used in court should she decide to prosecute. An emergency room physician noted,

> When a rape victim comes to see me or calls me, I try to get her to have the exam because six months from now she may decide she wants to prosecute. The first thing I tell her is don't shower, don't change clothes, and urinate in a cup. If the rape occurred more than seventy-two hours earlier, a full rape workup can't be done.

A survivor may find her way to the emergency room by way of the police, a friend, or a rape crisis hot line worker. In some instances, she may go to her family physician later to treat the injuries or make sure she is okay. As stories from survivors indicate, the police have considerable influence over the woman's decision whether to have the examination. If the investigator believes that he or she has a valid case that is prosecutable, he or she will likely encourage the woman to go to the emergency room and may, in fact, accompany her there. If, however, as illustrated by Debbie's story, the survivor is initially discouraged from filing a complaint, it is unlikely that she will pursue medical attention as a first course of action. It is noteworthy that Debbie had numerous cuts and scratches indicative of force that were never photographed, documented, or treated. In addition, considerable physical trauma and a violation of her genitals and rectum had occurred over the many hours of sexual assault she endured. When she finally did get police attention, it was too late to be able to use physical evidence in the prosecution of her assailant.

If a woman goes to the emergency room before contacting the police, the hospital must report the crime, as it is required by law to report all violent crimes of which it has knowledge. The woman's name and address, the nature and extent of her injuries, and the location of the assault must appear in this report. This may take the choice away from the survivor about whether to get the police involved. She has just been made powerless by her attacker, who has taken away her fundamental freedom of choice over the use of her body. The consequent lack of freedom of choice to report may feel like a second rape. In any event, if a woman is aware that the hospital will report the crime, this may act as a deterrent to seeking help from the emergency room, which is usually the place most equipped to handle rapes.

Private physicians, who must protect patient-doctor privileged communication, are not mandated to report violent crimes to the police. For this and other reasons, a survivor may feel more comfortable going to her own physician or gynecologist. If she plans to prosecute or is still considering it, however, she must make sure that correct and thorough evidence is collected. As far as we can determine, only hospital emergency rooms can do this.

The decision of where to go to seek medical attention presents somewhat of a dilemma to the survivor at a time when she is in crisis and not thinking clearly. A rape crisis counselor said,

> If a woman goes to the ER [emergency room] and doesn't want a crime report filed, we were told she should tell them she had had "rough sex." They will treat but won't collect the right evidence. You can't have it both ways. You can't collect evidence and *not* report it to the police.

The fear of the survivor, who needs time to gather her resources and find alternate plans for self-protection, is left unaddressed. One rape survivor reported,

> My landlord raped me, and a friend took me to the hospital. He'd blindfolded me so I couldn't see his face and threatened to kill me if I told anyone. A nurse said it looked like I'd been raped and that I should report it. I got off the table and left because I was so scared.

The best course of action is probably for the survivor to be truthful, notify the police, and collect the evidence. She can refuse to press charges or identify her attacker. She can buy time to be counseled about her options. She will probably be told that she has a lot of time within which she can decide to prosecute. This is true, but one wonders whether a change of heart will be viewed negatively by the police, the district attorney, and the jury. Certainly the defense attorney will use it against her.

Once the survivor makes the decision (or is urged to make the decision) to go to the hospital, the actual medical procedure is traumatic. Depending on the extent and severity of her physical injuries and how crowded the waiting room is, she may have to wait an uncomfortably long time, sometimes alone, until a physician or nurse practitioner can see her.

The survivor is often not informed about what will be done procedurally during the exam and why it is done. A fifty-year-old survivor said, "I had an exam that lasted about one-half hour. I knew the doctor would be collecting evidence, but I wish a nurse had better prepared me for it." Because the rape survivor has just had every ounce of control taken from her during the assault, it is understandable that she would like to have more control during the exam. To be the passive object of others' actions must seem like a second rape.

The standard rape exam collects two types of evidence—physical evidence of the rape and the woman's medical history—both of which are extremely intrusive. A third type of evidence collected concerns details of the actual assault. First, specimens of physical evidence are collected for later analysis. Medical personnel scrutinize and probe the survivor's entire body, including her scalp and fingernails. Her outer body is examined for trauma to collect hairs, fibers, semen, and blood. A urine sample is requested for a baseline pregnancy test. During the gynecological part of the exam, medical personnel may need to take a swab of the cervical canal if the assault occurred more than six hours before the exam. The physician also examines anal skin and inspects for anal penetration. The woman must indeed feel that once again her body is not her own. Many, if not most, women dislike these procedures even under the best circumstances.

Medical personnel are looking for evidence related to the use of force and penetration, materials originated from the assailant, and materials related to the location of the assault. Evidence can be collected and released only with the woman's signed consent. If photographs are taken, an additional consent is required. Lydia, a stranger rape survivor, told us, "I really didn't want photographs taken. I couldn't bear the thought of anyone else seeing me like that."

The second type of evidence collected pertains to the survivor's medical history. Besides her general health, medical staff may ask her about her gynecological history. They will want to know whether she has had any symptoms of pregnancy, the type of contraception she uses, and whether voluntary intercourse had occurred at any time in the four days prior to the assault. When questioning her on the circumstances of the assault, they ask the date, time, and location. At this point in the exam, they question the survivor about her previous use of alcohol or drugs, an item of concern to the police.

Questions about the assault per se include the number of assailants; the use of threats, weapons, or physical force; and the injuries sustained. They may want to know whether the woman injured her assailant and whether there was penetration—vaginally, anally, or orally. They ask whether ejaculation occurred and where and whether the assailant used a condom. Lastly, the survivor is asked about her activities since the assault—whether she has changed her clothes, douched, bathed, or washed, used mouthwash, eaten, drunk, urinated, defecated, or used medication or alcohol. All of this takes place while the woman is in a state of extreme trauma.

Blood specimens for alcohol or drug levels are taken only if clinically indicated or requested by law enforcement officers. An emergency room physician noted, "The physician has a choice about drug and alcohol screens, and these are controversial. Some doctors like to use them, and defense attorneys can use the results on the suspect's behalf."

We cannot help but wonder how police or physicians arrive at a decision about whether to test for alcohol or drugs, since the survivor is not the one who committed the crime. We wonder whether this procedure is in her best interest. Once again, it appears to be out of her hands. It would seem to contribute only to a case against her no matter how slight the ingestion. In contrast, the suspect's drug or alcohol level at the time of the crime is rarely tested and is only a matter of the survivor's word during the trial.

The victim also must make decisions regarding pregnancy, venereal disease, and acquired immunodeficiency syndrome (AIDS). If pregnancy is possible, she has three options: to wait and see, then have an abortion; to have a menstrual extraction (D and C); or to use postcoital drug contraception. Since diethylstilbestrol (DES), the most commonly prescribed "morning after" pill, causes nausea in many women and has been known to be a cancer-causing agent under certain circumstances (Burgess and Holmstrom 1979), none of the choices are without risk or uncomfortable side effects.

For venereal disease, the survivor has two options. She may have an immediate prophylactic treatment (penicillin, ampicillin, or tetracycline) or have follow-up tests for gonorrhea in two weeks and syphilis in six weeks. The threat of dangerous sexually transmitted diseases no doubt exacerbates the victim's fear and trauma.

In recent years, more and more survivors are becoming frightened of the deadly specter of AIDS as the aftermath of rape. Gonorrhea may be dangerous, but AIDS is fatal. And the fear that AIDS could be transmitted during rape is not without some basis. Rapists may be in a high-risk category for Human Immunodeficiency Virus (HIV). As a group, they may be partial to behaviors associated with the transmission of AIDS, such as intravenous (IV) drug use and anal intercourse. Although opposing information would suggest that rapists may inadvertently practice safe sex (by wearing a condom to avoid leaving a semen sample) and that people are unlikely to contract AIDS from a single exposure, these facts do little to assure the survivor in the absence of testing (Saholz et al. 1990).

Legal battles are being waged over who—the survivor or the rapist—must bear the responsibility for being tested for AIDS. As of this writing, only eight states have passed statutes requiring mandatory testing of sex crime defendants or convicted rapists. In most other states, the courts are maintaining that it is the survivor's problem. If the rapist does consent to be tested, it is often used as a bargaining chip. In one case in New York City, a rapist was promised a reduced sentence in exchange for submitting to an AIDS test and providing his victim with the results. What are the ramifications if the rapist does test positive? In New Orleans, a district attorney attempted, unsuccessfully, to have first-degree murder charges brought against an HIV-positive rapist (Saholz et al. 1990).

Whether or not the attorneys have information about the rapist's HIV status, it does little good legally for the woman to be tested. Even if she is found to be carrying the AIDS virus, the defense attorney will no doubt try to prove that she got the disease from someone else. If the survivor wants to be tested, she may have to pay for the testing herself and, if she is so unfortunate as to test positive, for the medical treatment as well. She also may be discriminated against by insurance companies, some of which have been accused of penalizing people who even take the test. Thus, AIDS is a second rape of the highest magnitude, considering that a woman's very life is at stake (Saholz et al. 1990).

Given the circumstances under which the survivor arrives at the hospital and the trials she must endure while there, the medical personnel whom she encounters should be as concerned and sympathetic as they would be under any life-threatening emergency. As one emergency room physician told us, "A physician needs to develop trust and rapport before asking the sensitive questions."

Yet despite the forensic equipment at their disposal, the physician on call or the medical personnel who interview the survivor may be uninformed about rape trauma. One rape survivor reported, "The doctor was cold. There was not one word of comfort from the man. At the end of the exam, he was going to give me Valium. I said, 'You SOB, I'm depressed enough. I don't want a depressant.'"

Many police departments now have mandatory classes to teach their personnel about rape crisis intervention, but this is not the case with hospitals. The emergency room physicians we interviewed stated that they had had no specific training in rape or crisis intervention. This is not to say that no hospitals in the country have appropriate hospital protocol. We know of at least one hospital that has a training guide outlining procedural issues and considerations for the emotional well-being of rape survivors.

A hospital is a major force in either aiding the survivor or causing greater distress. It would behoove all medical personnel who might have contact with rape survivors to understand the rape trauma syndrome. As with the police, the survivor is very sensitive to any intimation of blame coming from medical personnel.

The mother of a fourteen-year-old rape survivor reported, "Despite the fact that my daughter had evidence of force, the MD (a woman) took me aside and said, 'Don't you let your daughter date older men.'" This girl, who was either learning disabled or borderline retarded, was raped by a man in his forties who was a family friend and an elder in their church. Not only was the teenager traumatized by the sexual assault, but the mother was as well. The mother concluded, "I think she (the doctor) drew the wrong conclusion about what my daughter meant based on this limited contact. It was as if she were pointing out that I was a bad mother." Clearly, tactless, judgmental comments from medical personnel go a long way toward inflicting a second rape.

Discrepancies between a medical report and a police report may present problems in court. That was the case in the rape of the fourteen-year-old girl mentioned previously. The mother said, "The doctor accused my daughter of *not* being raped because her description of the time sequence was off or something." As it turned out, the police decided not to prosecute this case, although they did believe the rape had occurred. The girl would not have made a good witness, we were told, because of her intellectual limitations and the error she had unintentionally made in giving the time sequence during the medical exam. The family became discouraged about this treatment, the church's position in protecting the suspected assailant, and a victim advocate who kept pointing out the discrepancy in facts. They left their jobs and school and relocated across the country.

In the final analysis, a medical record does not contain any conclusions about whether a sexual assault occurred. Physical evidence is collected, and with the survivor's signed consent, it is released to law enforcement officials to be analyzed by a crime lab. If the survivor is ambivalent about going forward with prosecution, she can consent to the collection of evidence but withhold consent for its release until a later date.

In terms of the survivor's history, medical staff should obtain and record only information that is relevant to her medical care and medicolegal evidence collection requirements. Obviously, overlooking a major medical need of the survivor is a second rape. A fifty-year-old survivor noted, "My face was bruised and swollen, but the emergency room doctor didn't bother to x-ray my head. I later learned from my own physician that I had a broken nose." Questions that relate to a woman's reasons or motivations for her behavior, such as "Why did you go out at night?" are totally inappropriate and a second rape as well.

Evidence collection kits can be purchased commercially. They contain instructions and the materials needed to collect, label, and preserve specimens. These kits can be supplied by local law enforcement officials or prepared by physicians.

The authors wondered why more private physicians do not have these kits at their disposal. One reason is that preparing for court testimony takes a lot of time. In addition, some physicians do not want to testify in court. One emergency room physician told us, "For court testimony, I spend a lot of time reviewing the literature. My work, my reports, my testimony is perfectionistic. District attorneys are used to doctors who are scared to death."

Physicians also need to take time off from work to testify, resulting in the loss of patient income. The low pay for performing rape exams also is a factor. One emergency room physician said, "Most of the time I get paid $80 by the hospital for an exam. I'm paid very poorly for doing these. Last year I saw nineteen rape victims. . . . I think I should definitely be paid for being on call."

The physicians we interviewed stated that they think it is a good idea to have a nurse or a patient advocate assigned to provide support to the survivor in the hospital. Most agreed that emergency rooms need to eliminate the long wait most victims must endure. They also seemed to think that the core problem lies in the decision about whether to do an exam. One physician said, "The victim does not make the decision about the exam if she decides to report. We do not make this decision either. The police detective is the one with all the power to say whether an exam is done or not."

Unfortunately, medical personnel are not always in the service of the survivor. They are only one link in a chain of command that abides by society's myths and treatment of rape, and they can cause grave harm in the process.

# 10

# The Criminal Justice System

**A** survivor's motives for wanting to press charges and see her assailant be prosecuted are generally well founded in light of what she's just been through. She may, like most of us, subscribe to the belief that a wrong against her will be punished by our justice system, which exists to protect her rights as a U.S. citizen and to keep the world safe. As the survivor stories in chapters 3–6 indicate, many survivors must forcibly restrain their anger as they wait for justice to be served.

Mercedes said, "I have fantasies about cutting off his dick and balls. I knew I couldn't take the law into my own hands, so prosecuting was the only legal way I felt that I could get any satisfaction."

Lydia noted, "The extent of my anger scared me. Never in my life had I felt such hate for another human being. I had dreams of killing him. I wish I had jammed my fingers into his eyes."

Other survivors are motivated by a sense of community. They report the crime to prevent the victimization of other women and children. "I just couldn't stand the thought of him doing this to other women, so I had to follow this through. I felt he had done it before and he would do it again," Mercedes told us.

One of the most predominant motives for the survivor's desire to prosecute is fear. This emotion is almost universally felt after rape trauma, and the alleviation of this intense and debilitating state is sought by means of prosecution. Hear what survivors have to say:

> I couldn't even go out of my apartment without getting so scared I would throw up. Going to the grocery store was an ordeal.

They had my purse with my driver's license, which meant they knew where I lived. I spent two days just lying in my dark closet.

I just knew he would come back to find me, to try to shut me up forever, so I had to try to put him behind bars.

Every time I would see a car that looked like his, I started shaking. I was so scared that he would try to silence me. I could sleep better if I knew he was behind bars.

Despite a woman's desire to prosecute, she may be discouraged by the police or the district attorney. As we learned in chapter 8, the police may decide not to file a complaint. Although training and attitudes in police departments have improved since the late 1960s, a criminal court judge admitted that two women may be treated differently: "A woman who is cruising with the idea of going to bed with a guy will not be treated as seriously in her complaint. This doesn't mean they don't believe she was raped or that they don't like the person."

If the survivor's complaint does reach the district attorney's office, it may be stopped there for a variety of reasons. Usually the survivor is blamed for this decision, as her story is scrutinized for consistency. A female prosecutor said, "We always interview rape victims before we file. We see how consistent they are. We look for how accurately their report matches the police report."

Several survivors told us that their initial police report was wrong. Either they were so shaken that they forgot essential details or the police officer didn't copy down the information correctly. When the prosecutor is interviewing the woman, she may not be in such a state of shock, in reflection may remember forgotten details, and in general is calmer the second time around. Pointing out inconsistencies and failing to prosecute for that reason leaves the survivor feeling that she has been raped again.

Sometimes the woman is blamed because she intentionally conceals evidence due to embarrassment and humiliation. One prosecutor noted, "Some women exaggerate and say they were kidnapped because they feel embarrassed to call it rape, especially if they know their attacker."

Other survivors admitted that they added a weapon to their account so that they would be believable. One prosecuting attorney stated that he felt it was good policy to inform the survivor of what the consequences of concealing information can be. He stated that it was part of being a good attorney to build rapport so that a witness can be truthful.

All the prosecuting attorneys interviewed stated that it is imperative that the raped woman be completely open and honest, which includes relating whether there has been a relationship in the past, whether consensual sex had occurred in the past, and whether alcohol or drugs were present. One prosecutor said,

> I've had a lot of rape cases crumble because clients don't tell me the complete truth, so knowing this in advance is very important to me. I also want to know if she reported right away. If she waited too long, especially in a date rape, I don't file.

Survivors are in a catch-22. Any hesitancy in reporting and any omission of details or the slightest commission of a falsehood that is discovered will be used against the survivor and can be cause for not prosecuting. Alternatively, a woman who is honest and open may find her case rejected as well.

Stranger cases are easier to prosecute, but one attorney stated, "About half of the people know each other. Even if she has just seen him at the local grocery, he is not a stranger. The less the relationship between victim and attacker, the easier it is to have the jury with you."

Defense attorneys may go to great lengths to insist that the parties knew each other and to put the case in the category of acquaintance rape. For instance, since Mercedes lived in the same general neighborhood as her attacker, the defense counsel tried to make the jury believe that they knew each other. A superior court judge related the case of an aerobics instructor who described a man who jumped out of the bushes and attacked her as she was going to a movie. The woman claimed that the man, whom she called a stranger, raped her in the parking lot, then kidnapped her, took her to her home, and raped her again. Most of the defense's case was built on the fact that these two people had worked at the same location several years previously. In his far different version, the alleged assailant stated that they were acquainted and that she was attracted to him and receptive to his advances.

In criminal cases, a jury must be convinced beyond a reasonable doubt that the crime occurred and that it was committed by the defendant. This puts a lot of pressure on the district attorney's office to come up with a foolproof case. Obviously, any connection between the survivor and the defendant makes the case weaker, and this factor is always present in the decision-making process of whether to prosecute. A criminal court judge stated, "I have the impression that the DA's office is more eager to issue cases now than in the past. Date rape cases would have been rejected, but now they're probably resolved short of trial. I've never heard a date rape case." The judge is referring to the popular occurrence of plea bargaining in even the strongest of date rape cases.

A survivor's history of consensual sex with her attacker will make the case difficult to prove beyond a reasonable doubt. It is very easy, as in Debbie's attack, to say that the woman just got tired of the man and cried rape when she actually consented. This case was plea-bargained even though the police had obtained a confession from Debbie's ex-boyfriend.

The concept of plea bargaining in all rape cases will be discussed at length presently. Suffice it to say at this point that the prosecutor's scrutiny of a case in the beginning is traumatic for the survivor. Even the age of the survivor can be influential in the district attorney's decision whether to accept or reject a case. A male prosecutor noted, "Young girls and teenagers often fall apart. If a teen is attractive, dressed provocatively, has a sexually active dating history, or uses drugs, that will be used against her."

Mercedes's appearance as an attractive, mature-looking woman with long blond hair and her dating history were used by the defense attorney to incriminate her. They also tried to insinuate that she was a drug user and that she was molested as a child. Neither of these allegations was true, but a jury's prejudgments about the immorality of today's teenagers carry a lot of weight.

Apparently, a really strong case occurs when the survivor is severely injured physically during the rape. In Lydia's case, her pubic hairs were burned and her nose was broken. Although she tried to fight off her attacker, she was not successful. At the other extreme is Mercedes's case. She fought her attacker and escaped serious injury. Had she not been so skilled in self-defense, however, the crime would have been more believable because she would have had the injuries to prove it. As it was, the case was tried, but the defendant was found not guilty. Katie did not struggle due to the intimidation and rank of her attacker. Many people, including her mother, blamed her for not fighting back.

Thus, it appears that women can't win. They are punished by the system whether they fight back or don't fight back. But if they almost lose their life or sustain serious injuries, they have a strong case. Aggressive, self-protective women are at a disadvantage if they were not seriously injured. The goal, one might assume, is not to be *too* successful. The myth that a *real* victim should be found lying crumpled on the ground in a pool of blood is still alive and well.

The district attorneys we interviewed unanimously stated that the burden of proof lay with them—not the defense—in rape cases. It is very difficult to get a guilty verdict in these cases because of the bias with which we view rape in our society. When an attorney decides to file charges against a rape suspect, he or she must consider how a not guilty verdict would affect his or her career. A female prosecutor said,

> There is tremendous pressure on us to win every case. We are using the taxpayers' dollars to try a case, and there are too many complaints to take all of them to trial. This win mentality makes prosecutors reluctant to proceed with cases that have a low possibility of conviction.

One of her male counterparts added, "It's as simple as this: district attorneys refuse a case if they don't think it's convincing. Our egos and reputations are at hand. We like to win."

Unfortunately, survivors are often led to believe that a failure to prosecute has to do with something they did wrong when in reality the problem is a system that politically and economically is prejudiced against prosecuting rape. Prosecutors should base their decisions about filing cases on the written standards of their offices, not on whether they think they will win or lose. But that is not how it works.

To add to a woman's despair, she is often not even told the reason why the prosecutor dropped her case. Only one female prosecutor that the authors interviewed felt that if she decided not to file a case, she needed to explain her reasons to the survivor. The other attorneys did not agree.

The authors asked what a survivor could do if she still wanted to prosecute. Some of the prosecutors said that there was nothing she could do, but others said that she could try to go to the district attorney's supervisor or the press. This tactic may, however, work against the survivor. One prosecutor said, "You don't really want to piss off the DA because you very well could be stuck with that person and you want him or her on your behalf."

If the prosecutor refuses to take the survivor's case, it makes her feel even more helpless and powerless than she already feels. Not filing a case can be like granting a license to the attacker to commit another crime. We know of a number of survivors who have been assaulted by suspects who had been accused of other rapes, but against whom cases were not filed.

Assuming that the attorney for the state does decide to prosecute, the survivor has a lot more to face from that point on. Many people think that she just appears in court once and tells her story, and the rapist is behind bars. The media also lead the public to believe that there is only a short time between the crime and the trial. Nothing could be further from the truth. This time span varies from jurisdiction to jurisdiction, but a conservative estimate of the time from the date of the crime to the date of the sentencing is anywhere from six months to two years. A survivor of rape by a neighbor reported,

> The first time they prosecuted, it was only six months from the date of the crime until the trial. But then they had a hung jury. Then I went through a year and a half of sheer agony as time after time the retrial was postponed. Fortunately, he was found guilty, but the whole process ate up two years of my life.

Although procedures vary slightly from state to state, usually the first place the survivor must appear in the legal arena is at the arraignment or preliminary hearing. There a judge determines whether there is sufficient evidence to bind the suspect, who has just been arrested, over for trial. The survivor, who is now called a witness for the state, and possibly other witnesses may be called upon to testify. They can be cross-examined by the counsel for the suspect, who is now called the defendant. This counsel may be a court-appointed or private attorney. If the judge finds sufficient evidence, or probable cause, the case is scheduled for trial in a higher court. The defendant is either jailed or released on bail (based on whether he has a record for felonies). If the case is not bound over for trial, it is dismissed.

Many survivors stated that they wished they had been better prepared for the preliminary hearing by their counsel. Lydia said, "I didn't know that my attacker would have to walk up close to me, take off his shirt, and show the scars on his back. I felt as if I would throw up." A survivor of a stranger gang rape reported,

> I was so terrified of my attacker that the attorneys worked out an agreement so that he could hide in the witness box while I testified. I didn't learn that he'd been there until later. If I'd had to face him, I wouldn't have been able to do it.

Sometimes it is a shock for the survivor to realize that her attacker will be sitting in front of her at the hearing. It may not be possible to prepare the survivor psychologically for the arraignment because it can occur very soon after the initial report. The defendant is entitled to hear everyone's testimony so as to rebut it later. The survivor is a witness and is allowed in the courtroom only while she is testifying. Many survivors remarked that this was when they first realized that it was not their trial, that the attacker's rights were the ones being protected, and that they had had no control over what happened to their bodies. The structure of the system often results in a second rape.

Between the arraignment and trial, the prosecutor and the defense attorney may engage in plea bargaining. Plea bargaining is an attempt by our criminal justice system to weigh the evidence on both sides and make a decision about the crime and sentence without having to go through the long process of a jury trial. The state and the defense must agree to a plea bargain for it to be successful. It is then presented to the judge as a resolution of the case. Typically the defendant is talked into pleading guilty to a lesser related offense and receiving the sentence in accord with the lesser offense. For instance, in Debbie's case, although five charges were initially brought against her attacker (including rape), after plea bargaining, he pled guilty only to attempted rape.

Many of the district attorneys we interviewed were very much in favor of plea bargaining for a variety of reasons. Much depends on the strength of the state's case—the evidence that speaks on the survivor's behalf and her emotional state. Remember that Debbie had no medical evidence of rape and had had a prior consensual relationship with the defendant. These factors weakened her case, and thus plea bargaining was attempted. Other attorneys said that with overcrowded courts and the unpredictability of jurors' attitudes about rape, plea bargaining is often preferable to trial for the survivor. One prosecutor noted,

> Plea bargaining can be to a woman's advantage because the rape victim may not get total justice from the legal system. They might be helped if they viewed an actual trial. They just keep telling and retelling their story, and all the time everyone is scrutinizing. Rape cases also take more time than burglary cases, and there is a stiffer sentence.

Another said, "I think plea bargaining is a good idea when the years of prison make sense." A criminal court judge had this to say:

> I don't like the words *plea bargaining* because they make it sound like someone is getting away with something. I prefer the words *case settlement*. Both sides realistically assess the liability they have in going to trial. For the victim, it's better to get something than nothing. The attorneys try to convince the victim or the defendant to work out an arrangement. The defense attorney tells his or her client to plead guilty, which he's not happy about. The bargain is for society, and the DA's responsibility is to society.

Despite the fact that the system obviously leans toward plea bargaining, the survivor often experiences it as a second rape because she views it as a betrayal. Many survivors report feeling cheated, especially if they have not been consulted or have been misled. It is interesting to note that in misdemeanor cases, the survivor (now the plaintiff) has the control, but in felonies such as rape, the survivor may be left out of the decision to plea-bargain. In California, victim's rights legislation passed in 1981 requires that the victim of a crime be consulted about plea bargaining. This does not, however, mean that she has any real input. One survivor noted, "I was informed they were plea bargaining my case through a letter in the mail. My DA didn't even have the decency to talk with me about it." This woman's statement reflects the confusion of most survivors about the process. It is neither *her* case nor *her* attorney.

A survivor of an attempted rape told us, "I was finally told that there would not be a trial because he'd pled guilty to false imprisonment. I wasn't consulted until after the fact." Another woman said, "He either raped me or he didn't. What is all this other garbage? When they told me about their bargain, they actually made it sound like it was good news."

The prosecutors we interviewed vary in the degree to which they allow survivors to influence plea bargaining. One said, "I always try to include the victim's opinions and desires when considering a plea bargain." But another reported, "Plea bargaining is not really the victim's choice. We'll listen to her, but we can override her."

Survivors usually are told that it is in their best interest to plea bargain so as to avoid the horrors of a trial and because they don't have a strong case. In reality, plea bargaining is the way our criminal justice system has of unloading some of its more easily settled cases. There are too many complaints for the system to handle, and it costs a lot of money to bring a case to trial. Thus, plea bargaining is based on political and economic reasons and has little to do with the survivor.

A case can be plea-bargained at any time, even after the trial has begun. Therefore, a survivor may be mentally preparing for a trial for a long time. She is exposed to three specific aspects of victimization by the judicial proceedings: delays, the public setting, and the treatment of the victim as if she were the offender (Burgess and Holmstrom 1979).

Numerous delays and postponements are the rule rather than the exception in the court process. Many survivors report that they put their lives on hold until it's all over, at which time they can go on living. We have never met a survivor who took a pending court trial lightly and didn't to some degree become obsessed with it. Survivors arrange their lives around appointments with the prosecutor or court dates, only to have them canceled at the last minute. Hours are lost from work, which can aggravate an already stressful situation. Survivors often lose income, and there may be extra costs for transportation or baby-sitters. The survivor must mentally and emotionally prepare for each scheduled interview or testimony. Lengthy preparation is spent in counseling, reliving the assault (which is very painful), and summoning the psychological strength to go through the ordeal of a trial.

Survivors told us that sometimes they would show up in court and wait several hours expecting to testify, only to find out from the court clerk that the trial had been moved to a later date. Each time a woman is let down like this, especially when she is not notified by the prosecutor, she feels as though she has been raped again.

Court delays exist because prosecutors are overloaded with work, courtrooms are overbooked, and hundreds of cases are backlogged. Delays also can be a defense tactic. It's often to the defendant's advantage to postpone a trial and ask the judge for a continuance. In Lydia's case, the proceedings were canceled several times. One postponement was due to the incomplete psychological evaluation of her attacker. A second postponement was due to the rapist's request for a different defense attorney. The latter is a common excuse. It is ironic that the defendant can request a new attorney but it is next to impossible for the survivor to get a new one. Even if she created a scene and was granted a new attorney, the system might look on this unfavorably.

Delays, regardless of their intent, wear down the survivor. The more exhausted and frustrated she becomes, the more likely it is that she will leave town and become "lost." A survivor does not have the right to cease a prosecution just because she has changed her mind, but she can act in such an uncooperative way that the prosecution is dropped. One survivor became so exhausted by the time her case was scheduled for trial for the third time that she went to Europe to recuperate, and the case was dropped. The law says that courts should weigh the impact of a delay on the victim against the defendant's rights before granting a continuance. What the law dictates and what really occurs are two different things.

Once the trial takes place—perhaps a year or a year and a half after the crime—other sources of stress in the courtroom confront the survivor. Rape trials usually are not closed to the public unless the survivor is very young. Spectators may be present. The survivor will be asked to state her name and address and to give detailed accounts of sexual acts before total strangers. The survivor cannot speak quietly, as there is a microphone in front of her and a court reporter taking down every word. This is, of course, in addition to the treatment she receives from the defense attorney, which is intended to discredit her in any way possible.

We interviewed several male defense attorneys, who expressed points of view considerably different from those of the district attorneys. They were all surprisingly likable in light of the stories we'd heard about the brutal defense tactics used against witnesses in the courtroom. Both private and state (public defender) attorneys said that they would not accept a client under suspicion of rape if they found him personally repugnant. In general, however, they liked defending rapists. "I always have spoken for the underdog," one defense attorney stated, referring to the defendant rather than the victim.

This attitude is indirectly connected to the myth that rape is a crime where some poor, unsuspecting soul is unjustly accused by a vengeful, evil, or at least stupid woman. Many popular courtroom television dramas also feed into this myth. Usually the hero is the defense attorney, who through skillful investigative techniques and clever cross-examination gets the unjustly accused client released week after week. As a society, we tend to identify with and root for the underdog. But we know of no dramas that depict a person being set free when he or she really did commit a crime.

One defense attorney stated, "The truth is not attainable to any of us. It's all subjective." This is another version of the oft-repeated line "It's just her word against his." That means that a woman would have just as much reason to make up a rape as a man would have to deny it. But it would seem that a suspect would have greater motivation to lie than an accuser. After all, he, not she, faces possible incarceration, fines, and loss of family, friends, and job if found guilty. Neither would a woman benefit from the attention and feedback of the court process.

Maybe it does come down to which side can present the best case. A suspect who can afford a private practice attorney often has an advantage. The overworked and perhaps underpaid prosecutor and public defender often are too busy juggling cases to give any rape case the same kind of attention a private practitioner can. That is not to say that these attorneys are less qualified than private practitioners, but they just don't have the time to devote to each case.

Our society is more able to tolerate a guilty person walking free than the conviction of an innocent person. The defense attorneys we interviewed mentioned several tactics used to make the jurors believe that they may be sending the wrong man to prison. In a stranger rape case, they stir up doubts about the identity of the survivor's attacker. This may be done by asking her if she had just seen a picture of the man she accused or she had just seen him in the local supermarket or in the neighborhood.

Attorneys also admitted to spending considerable time in cross-examination attempting to expose inconsistencies in the survivor's testimony. One public defender said, "I try to expose inconsistencies in her story, especially date circumstances. I ask whether she had opportunities to escape, because consent makes her position more difficult. Inconsistency creates suspicion of the woman." Each time a defense attorney can punch a hole in a survivor's story, it has the effect of making the jury believe she doesn't really know what she's talking about or is not a very good liar. All it takes is a few inconsistencies to plant a reasonable doubt.

The defense's case is strengthened by reliable character witnesses willing to testify on behalf of the accused. In Mercedes's case, her attacker's boss and pastor were present, telling the jury of his superb performance and untainted past. Juries also place considerable weight on the suspect's appearance and background. "Most wives stand by their husbands because they want to believe in them," one attorney said. "If you have a wife who is pregnant and he looks like a clean-cut family man, the jury will find it more difficult to believe that he is a rapist."

Survivors often report that they feel defensive when they are testifying. This blaming the victim is a common courtroom tactic. One survivor explained,

> It felt like he was trying to get the jury to believe I had done something wrong, like I was the one on trial. He kept talking about how I wear shorts when I water my lawn—like I was a prostitute and

sending out invitations. I kept telling myself that he was just doing his job, but I felt so demeaned I broke down and cried.

The aforementioned aerobics instructor case was related to us by several attorneys. It illustrates the various issues on which attorneys focus to blame the victim. One version is as follows:

> Mr. Jones, the accused, was married with children and held down a stable job. On the day in question, a muggy fall afternoon, he was off work and visiting friends. He was walking toward his car when he made eye contact with the accuser, Ms. Doe, who was on her way to a movie. *He thought he recognized her.* She smiled and they had a brief conversation. He advanced, and she was receptive. They had oral and vaginal sex in a secluded but public area near the parking lot. *All this time, they were two to three blocks from the sheriff's station. In fact, several people went by and looked in their direction.* He shielded her. *She did not scream or attempt to get away.* He walked the girl several blocks home, and she invited him inside. They had sex again in her living room and then *a discussion about Christian beliefs.* He started to leave, and she offered him a ride to his car. He declined and left. *She didn't call for help or contact anyone.* She was not crying or upset.
>
> She went back and saw the movie. Later that night, she went home and called her pastor, with whom she was smitten. She went to see him, and they had a long conversation during which she told him she had been attacked. The wife of the pastor with whom Ms. Doe was studying, a rape victim herself, told her she'd been raped. *Five to six hours after her attack, she called the police. There were no physical signs of trauma.*

The various issues, italicized above, are as follows:

1. They knew each other, so she could have consented.
2. She didn't struggle, scream, or call for help despite numerous opportunities during and immediately following the rape.
3. The woman didn't report the incident to the police until many hours later.
4. She may have claimed rape to avoid punishment by her church (a guilty conscience).
5. There were no physical signs to suggest nonconsensual sex.

In the survivor's version of the rape, the suspect, a total stranger, jumped out at her from behind the bushes. He threatened her with a pocketknife, which was why she didn't scream. Like so many survivors, she acted ambivalently about whether she had been violated, and it took encouragement for her to act. Shock and immobilization are part of the rape trauma and in this case were used against the survivor—a second rape.

The defense may expose the woman's sexual reputation, her general character, and her emotional state at the time of the incident. Let's continue with Ms. Doe's case from the defense's point of view.

She was attractive, with a presentation of a demure Christian woman. At the trial she dressed to present the image of a virgin. She cried on the stand, carried a Bible, and wore a cross for all to see. She expressed her belief in God on the stand. But information was sought about her real background to see if she was what she wanted to appear.

It was learned that she had recently taken a rape seminar with her mother. She knew what to do, yet she took a shower and destroyed the evidence. She didn't even call her mother, who lived only a few blocks away. She was a strong, physically fit woman, yet she never fought back. We also discovered that she had recently broken up with her boyfriend. She called him to say she'd been violated, perhaps to gain his sympathy and win him back. She was attracted to her recently single pastor and worried about her reputation in the church. She had many reasons to make this into a rape. Unfortunately, there can no longer be a polygraph or a psychological evaluation on victims.

On the other hand, Mr. Jones had no history of criminal contact. They were exposed to each other several years previously. He was somewhat of a ladies' man, but even Mrs. Jones stated that it was ridiculous that her husband would have to rape in this day and age. There probably was rough sex between the two, but then violence can be part of sex play. A jury isn't supposed to make value judgments about the man's behavior—just his guilt about the specific alleged crime. The main thing a jury must decide is if her story is logically consistent, and, quite honestly, it has more holes in it than Swiss cheese.

This case was of particular interest to us because of the contradictions and issues presented, all of which served to rape the survivor again. After two trials, two hung juries, and two years, Mr. Jones eventually pled guilty to a misdemeanor.

Consent is used in the defendant's favor when the man and woman are acquainted—no matter how they are acquainted—but especially if there are no physical injuries. It is incredible that even in Lydia's case, the attacker's defense attorney tried to allege consensual sex when she had a broken nose and burned pubic hairs.

Despite recent laws that you cannot bring out a survivor's past sexual history and morals, cannot polygraph her, and cannot suggest a psychological evaluation, these matters of her character and mental state can be addressed in a court of law more covertly. A public defender told us, "You can bring up a victim's morals only if she's lying. However, you can bring up her poor judgment always— like the way she was dressed or whether she was using alcohol or drugs."

Even if a woman's reputation is immaculate and her judgment perfectly sound, she must be on guard while on the stand, and she must always be consistent. Her police report, preliminary testimony, and trial testimony all must match. It is, at best, a nerve-racking, degrading experience. As a superior court chief justice stated, the result of making a victim a defendant is that "girls don't report rape for the humiliation involved in it, the degradation they go through in a trial" (Burgess and Holmstrom 1979, p. 302).

A discussion of our criminal justice system would be incomplete without mention of the jury, which is composed of twelve peers who must vote unanimously whether to return a verdict of guilty or not guilty. Prior to the trial and behind the scenes out of the survivor's presence, the jury has been chosen by the defense and the prosecution. The term for the questioning of prospective jurors is *voir dire*. It is a process of weeding out those persons who may not be impartial. Both the defense and the prosecution are allowed to excuse some potential jurors because of their suspected bias. One prosecutor said, "Younger people and college educated are the best to have on a jury because they are the most aware and educated about rape." But another reported, "My voir dire depends on whether it is a stranger or a date rape. I give them a myth and see how they react. With acquaintance rape cases, I tend to choose men for the jury. Women are much too critical of women."

From the prosecution's point of view, it would seem a young educated male would be the most unbiased. Prosecutors are looking for people who do not have any preconceived ideas about rape—people who do not have anything in their experience or background that would make it difficult for them to do the survivor and the defendant justice. Yet the socialization of both men and women includes preconceived ideas about rape, so this task must indeed be difficult. A defense attorney noted,

> The defense's job *must* be easier. I spent a lot of time on voir dire. I want to know if a juror could have been a victim or friend of a victim. I want to know if these people have been exposed to rape in any way—like if they work in a hospital.

It appears that empathy and knowledge of the crime must be screened out. In referring to the case of Mr. Jones, one defense attorney stated:

> There are two types of jurors—those who feel sorry for her and vote out of their emotions and those who are logical. They are only looking at the facts and feel no emotional connection. This is the kind of juror we're looking for.

A criminal court judge summed up jury selection this way:

> I believe that society's views have changed, but remember that a jury is a melting pot. For instance, things occur in other societies, and they're okay. In Laotian society, rape may be okay. District attorneys tend to be realistic and conservative. Their allegiance is to society, and society is not composed of people from a rape crisis center. They don't compose the jury. As far as jurors' attitudes, a woman with a miniskirt may have asked for it. Women can't go into certain types of bars without men assuming certain things. You can't turn off the spigot. Feminists mislead people. Men don't react the way they think they should. That only occurs in a perfect world, not the real world.

One final area in which survivors are raped for the second time is in sentencing, which occurs in the courtroom whether the case goes to trial or is plea-bargained. In most states, the survivor is allowed to speak at sentencing, although she may not be informed about this right. She can tell the judge how the assault has affected her life and what she feels is fair and just punishment for her attacker. This may, however, open the door for more attempts by the defense to humiliate and demean the survivor. It may bring her in touch with the psychological evaluation of the rapist, which can cause her more distress if she learns her attacker is not found dangerous. This point will be discussed at length in the next chapter.

But speaking at the sentencing also can make the survivor feel better. Lydia said, "That day in court when I got to speak, it was healing. I knew everyone in the courtroom was affected. The judge even had tears in his eyes." Deciding to prosecute also can be healing if a guilty verdict is the end result of a trial. The survivor has finally been validated by her peers, albeit at a high cost.

Unfortunately, betrayal and suspicion are part of the justice system's treatment of rape survivors. The state attorney's failure to prosecute, plea bargaining, and the monumental ordeal of going to trial are usually part of a second rape—no matter what the outcome.

# 11

# Mental Health Personnel

**M**ental Health personnel intervene with the rape survivor in various ways. Rape crisis programs and rape crisis hot lines (twenty-four-hour telephone response services) vary in availability from city to city depending on funding sources and the political atmosphere.

Some crisis workers are affiliated with police departments, some with hospitals, and some with community agencies. Training of these crisis workers varies depending on the particular affiliation of the group of workers being trained. For example, hospital personnel crisis workers may know how to help survivors with the immediate physical aspects of the crime, but they may know little about its emotional and legal ramifications. One survivor said,

> I really liked the nice woman who was at the hospital, and she talked with me about the rape, but I was in such a state of shock that I don't know if she was a social worker or what because I never saw her again. I wish there had been some follow-up.

Some hospital-based programs are designed to provide both immediate and long-term care of rape survivors. Emergency room staff may be specially trained and a specific protocol may be followed to ensure comprehensive medical treatment of a victim, with careful consideration of her legal needs and potential use of the medical record in a court of law (Burgess and Holmstrom 1979). In these emergency rooms, nursing staff see the survivor immediately upon admission and continue counseling follow-up. Most survivors we spoke with said that this approach is ideal. One said,

It would have been wonderful to have had someone by my side who knew about all aspects of the rape process from beginning to end. My psychologist was helpful when it came to coping emotionally, but she didn't know anything about the legal process. I didn't even get referred to her until a few weeks after the rape, and going through those first few weeks without support was torture.

Some community agencies have volunteers on call twenty-four hours a day, but they may be able to give only immediate assistance to help with the initial stages of the rape trauma syndrome (shock, fear, shame, and humiliation). One survivor was very pleased with the help she received:

I called the rape crisis hot line so much that I'm sure every worker there began to know me. I would often call at 2 or 3 A.M. after a frightening dream of the rapist or when I couldn't sleep. The hot line worker had a way of reassuring me that my feelings were normal and quite predictable for what I had gone through.

Another woman had opposite feelings about the help she received:

I think I would have been better off without a rape crisis worker. She was young enough to be my daughter, and she was so shocked about the horror of the crime that I felt as if I was taking care of her emotionally—like, you know, it was too much for her to hear.

Part of the problem with community volunteers and crisis intervention is that training can be excellent or deficient. A woman intervening with her first rape survivor is often surprised at the depth of her own feelings and may be unable to provide the support and confidence that the survivor needs. To see a rape survivor is to see the vulnerability within yourself. Often crisis workers become aware for the first time that rape could happen to them or someone they love. One crisis counselor stated,

On my first rape call, I approached the door of the survivor's home confidently, and within a few moments, my knees were weak. As the forty-year-old woman opened the door, she ran from the living room into her bedroom and sat inside her closet. I was not prepared for the extent of fear in her eyes, her disheveled appearance, or her little-girl, fragile expression. This woman had made the mistake of not locking her car doors while she was at the post office mailing Christmas packages. Her assailants were hiding in the backseat. Being in a hurry and not locking her doors changed her forever and almost cost her her life. I couldn't help but think how many times I had done the same thing—not locking my doors—but believe me, I lock them now.

Another crisis worker stated,

My first rape call is one I will never forget. I was called to the home of an eighty-six-year-old woman who was brutally raped with a knife held to her neck. I couldn't help but think of my own grandmother and how devastating a rape would be for her. I cried and shook with fear all the way home.

One problem with many women who volunteer for this type of crisis intervention is that they have been victims of rape or child sexual abuse themselves and overidentify with the survivor. According to one psychologist who specializes in training volunteers,

Many of my volunteers have never worked through their own victimization and subconsciously are drawn to this work. This in itself is not detrimental if she realizes that she needs her own individual therapy so that she may set her own limits and boundaries and not become overinvolved. Many of my volunteers, on a conscious level, may not even perceive themselves as rape survivors. Something in the rape counseling training experience may trigger a memory or an acknowledgment that they in fact had been raped at some point in their life. Or perhaps one of the women whom she counsels may trigger memories of her own victimization.

Some police departments are initiating community programs to deal with the problem of sexual assault. One program we know about is a social service agency that is part of the local police department. This program is a nonprofit public organization that provides emotional and practical support to victims of child abuse, sexual assault, domestic violence, and families of suicide and homicide victims. This program attempts to assist the survivor from the time the crime occurs until after prosecution if the case goes to court. The goal of the program is to provide consistency to the survivor in having one main support person follow her through the process. One counselor stated,

Someone needs to go through the entire process with the survivor not only to prepare her but to correct others' mistakes and careless comments. It is often what is said initially by helping professionals that can have long-term positive or negative effects on the survivor in her recovery.

This program often provides emotional support not only for the survivor of rape but also to her entire family. Family and friends, unsophisticated about what to say regarding the rape, can thwart a woman's recovery. For instance, a husband of one rape survivor had just returned from military duty overseas and could not understand why his wife was so inhibited sexually. "After all," he stated, "I'm not the rapist, so why can't she just get over it?"

This program also provides practical support in that it can assist the survivor with emergency transportation, food, and shelter. A survivor told us,

> I was raped while on my job, but my income was essentially cut in half even after I qualified for workmen's compensation. I would have lost my apartment and been without food if it hadn't been for some emergency funds. I have a child, too, and I'm single, so that was very frightening to me.

While the program is primarily a support agency for victims, it also conducts educational and prevention programs for children and teens. The premise of these programs is to teach children a sense of their own power and assertiveness, knowledge of safety and preventive measures, and available resources for support.

Another avenue for survivor help are the victim assistance programs that grew in the 1960s out of disillusionment with the long-term effectiveness of offender rehabilitation (Burgess and Holmstrom 1979). A number of different victim assistance models are used throughout the country. They have been developed to minimize the trauma of victimization by giving social service referrals and providing reimbursement through compensation.

Gaining in popularity is the prosecutorial model of victim assistance programs (Burgess and Holmstrom 1979). This model assumes that the responsibility for victim assistance lies with the prosecuting institution, since the victim is a witness for the state in its case against the defendant.

Many prosecutorial models of victim assistance include an intake screening process. The objective of the screening is to examine cases at the outset of the criminal proceeding in order to do the following (Burgess and Holmstrom 1979):

1. Screen out those cases in which the evidence is insufficient to warrant criminal prosecution
2. Screen out those cases in which the prosecution would not serve the best interest of the parties involved
3. Determine proper charges to be brought against the defendant
4. Establish effective, consistent case follow-up

This screening process can be distressing to the victim if it is not handled sensitively and if she is not prepared for the possible outcome. A survivor may have been given the erroneous information that all medical, psychological, or travel expenses would be covered. After her initial victim assistance screening, if her case doesn't qualify, she may feel like a failure, as though she has done something wrong. Furthermore, she may have the added stress of bills that she is unable to pay. Occasionally police or mental health professionals mislead survivors to believe that their cases will qualify for assistance but they don't. One survivor reported, "My psychologist, without hesitation, led me to believe my case would be covered by victim assistance, and then it wasn't. Now I have a large bill to pay for psychotherapy, and that is added stress for me."

Other mental health professionals who need specialized training to work with rape survivors are those who conduct individual therapy with those survivors. These people are usually psychologists, psychiatrists, social workers, or marriage, family, or child counselors. To work with a rape survivor appropriately, these professionals need to understand the typical reactions following a rape. One male psychologist received a call from a woman who was raped. Not knowing that the normal reactions include anger and hysteria, he was reluctant to take the woman into psychotherapy for fear that she had a serious personality disorder. He referred her to another, female psychologist. That decision was an ethical and intelligent one, since he had little training working with rape survivors.

Group psychotherapy can be particularly healing for rape survivors. In a group experience, they can see that other women have similar feelings. Many women need some prompting and encouragement to join a group because a normal reaction to assault may be self-imposed isolation. Another benefit of group work is that women can depersonalize their maltreatment by others when they see it occurring in various ways to others in the group. Of course, the group needs an experienced leader or therapist to facilitate healing, identify individual pathology, and help implement goals. Many women who were raped said that they were unable to locate rape recovery groups. In their opinion, backed up by information obtained from therapists, groups for incest and sexual molestation are more prevalent than rape groups.

One psychologist who runs several rape groups said that they are an absolute necessity for healing. "Many rape survivors have buried their experience for years and decide to come to a healing group after they have read a book on rape or seen a television special or movie about rape," she noted. "My rape groups are always full, and I have a waiting list for those who want to join."

To prevent further victimization of women, professionals can attend workshops that teach them how to deal with rape survivors. Police personnel and others who come in contact with survivors need to have some knowledge of the dynamics of rape as well as appropriate referrals for survivors.

The fact that so few programs follow survivors from the assault through recovery is another example of the second rape. Our society needs to spend sufficient time and money to develop caring programs for survivors.

Our discussion of mental health personnel would not be complete without including information and comments from forensic psychologists and psychiatrists who evaluate rapists, as well as opinions from survivors concerning those evaluations. Experts have debated whether rape is an act of violence or an act of sex. Nicholas Groth (1979) sees rape as the sexual expression of aggression rather than as the aggressive expression of sexuality. He describes three basic patterns of rape:

1. Anger rape, in which sexuality becomes a hostile act
2. Power rape, in which sexuality becomes an expression of conquest
3. Sadistic rape, in which anger and power become eroticized

Anger rape is characterized by physical brutality. More force is used on the victim than is necessary to achieve sexual penetration. The offender attacks his victim and usually is both physically and verbally abusive. His aim is to hurt and degrade his victim. Instead of just battering her, this man considers rape the ultimate offense he can commit. In some cases, he may urinate or defecate on her. The assault of the anger rapist is in response to some identifiable stress, such as an argument with his wife or girlfriend. Some assaults occur out of a sense of frustration.

In power rape, the offender wants to possess his victim sexually. This offender feels inadequate, and sexuality serves to express his mastery, strength, control, authority, identity, and capability. The amount of force may vary depending on situational factors, but he often becomes more aggressive over time. Frequently, this type of offender fantasizes about the sexual interaction, convincing himself that his victim complied. He needs to believe that she wanted or enjoyed it.

Power rape is the most frequent type of rape. It is also the type most easily dismissed by the legal system due to lack of physical injuries and the victim's familiarity with the offender. This is the type of rape that Debbie, Katie, and Mercedes suffered. This is also the type of thinking apparent in date or acquaintance rape.

In sadistic rape, sexuality and aggression become fused into sadism. Aggression becomes eroticized. The assault usually involves torture, and there is frequently a bizarre, ritualistic quality to it. The offender may subject his victim to peculiar actions. Lydia's rape was a sadistic one, as her offender wrote graffiti all over her body and burned her pubic hairs. The sadist reaches his peak of sexual excitement by inflicting pain on his victim, and the rape frequently results in the victim's death. Perhaps Lydia was correct when she said that she felt her offender would have killed her if she hadn't escaped.

As this description of rapists indicates, anger and power are common threads. It is difficult to generalize about rapists, so treatment strategies vary. Some mental health authorities favor imprisonment without treatment, others treatment without imprisonment.

Assessing the dangerousness of a rapist with the goal of determining incarceration versus outpatient rehabilitation is one task for a forensic psychologist or psychiatrist. This is a dubious task. The validity of being able to predict dangerousness has been seriously questioned.

According to experts (Cohen et al. 1978), a clinician should base his or her prediction of dangerousness on an extended period of study. In reality, this extended period of study often is cut to a two- to three-hour psychological interview with the use of some tests in a psychologist's or psychiatrist's office.

Ideally, the clinician should examine the offender's emotional, be-havioral, and psychological development through a detailed study of his social, sexual, educational, and vocational history, as well as his medical and psychological records and history of criminality. Part of this assessment should include interviews with the victim when possible.

Not one rape survivor whom we interviewed was included in the assessment of her attacker, and many felt angry about that fact. Debbie said, "I was never allowed to read the psychological evalu-ation, and the doctor never interviewed me. He could not have known Jim's threats to kill me or of his childhood history of brutal abuse. I knew he would hide all that from the doctor." A forty-one-year-old social worker who survived an attempted rape said,

> I kept telling my attacker's parole office that I felt he was dangerous, and he said he was evaluated by a court-appointed psychologist who felt differently. I was enraged. How could some psychologist deter-mine an answer to such an important question without even once hearing my side? I feel like I'm prey now. He's out on the street. He knows where I live, and he will probably be sentenced to attend ther-apy at some free clinic with a novice counselor. He'll come after me again—I just know it.

Forensic psychologists we interviewed admitted to less than per-fect evaluation techniques due to time limitations and monetary concerns. One psychologist said,

> The court pays us a certain amount for evaluations, so to make my work cost-effective, I can't take months to do it. Even though the offender may only spend two to three hours in my office, I interview everyone I can and review all available records. I would like to inter-

view the victim to see if there was threat and power used. I don't interview the victim because I always thought that going over the details of the rape again with some man whom she didn't know might be perceived as further victimization by her.

This psychologist felt that he was being sensitive to the survivor and protective of her by not talking with her about the rape. He related that he did try to talk with her therapist and glean details in that manner. Although this view is admirable, the survivors whom we interviewed related that they felt the evaluation would be less biased if their input was included.

In *Men Who Rape,* Nicholas Groth (1979) says that it is essential to examine the victim's version of what happened in the assault as compared to the offender's version. If the offender is interviewed without the evaluator knowing the victim's version, a number of important details may not be disclosed because of distortions in the offender's perception or because of deliberate falsification. If the clinician has both versions, he or she can determine what the offender can acknowledge, what he minimizes or distorts, and what he evades or denies.

According to research and experts in the field (Cohen et al. 1978), several factors should be addressed in assessing dangerousness and predicting response to treatment. Some of those factors are the nature of the aggressive impulse, the stimuli which elicit aggressive behavior, the discharge factors in such behavior, and the management of appropriate as opposed to violent aggression. These researchers indicated that even with these and other factors considered, the prediction of dangerousness is uncertain.

Ray Anderson (1990), director of the Sex Crimes Clinic in Van Nuys, California, told us that he feels that the "likelihood of recidivism of rape is high and that rape is not a crime that springs out of nowhere. There are usually steps that lead up to it, like breaking and entering a home where a woman lives alone, aggression, or battery of women." He sees a pattern of poor emotional bonding in the history of rapists and feels that a rape disorder is difficult to treat in the community. He acknowledged that most of his information is with the stranger rapist, who has a pattern of aggressive crimes against women.

When Dr. Anderson was asked about acquaintance or date rapists, he said that these men seldom get referred to him. "I believe there is more ambivalence on the part of judges in the acquaintance or date rape situation as to whether a rape actually occurred due to the consideration of victim participation," he noted. In addition, as Robin Warshaw (1988) discovered, these men seldom have a record, which makes them appear less dangerous and in less need of treatment. Acquaintance rapists appear to be just regular guys.

Most of the forensic psychologists we interviewed felt that drug or alcohol use could push the date or acquaintance rapist over the edge to commit a rape. One psychologist said, "I think most rapes start out as sexual and then get out of hand." According to forensic psychologist Reid Meloy (1989), "Stimulant drugs give the perpetrator an increased sense of entitlement, grandiosity, omnipotence, hypervigilance, and paranoia, thus perceived rejection and reduced empathy."

In contrast, Dr. Anderson (1990) said that drugs and alcohol play a rather minor role in the sexual and personal functioning of the recidivistic rapist. Nearly all of these highly recidivistic offenders are inclined to commit rape offenses with or without the disinhibiting influence of drugs or alcohol. The forces favoring the offense are urgent and obsessive rape fantasies, perceived (not necessarily real) sexual deprivation, and the intense high that these offenders feel during the commission of a crime.

Another forensic psychologist stated that in assessing dangerousness, he looks not only at aggressive acts but also at the kind of movies the man watches and his general orientation toward violence. Based on his experience of assessing many rapists, he said that transiency in employment and poor early parental bonding are red flags to look for in assessing dangerousness. He sees many rapists as having poor relationships with their father.

The treatment and rehabilitation of rapists also are cause for much debate. The public generally opposes allocation of money for treating rapists, whom they consider to be repulsive (Gelman et al. 1990). Programs that are in effect frequently use behavior modification techniques, such as administering mild shocks while inmates view pornographic rape material. Another treatment strategy is masturbatory reconditioning, which requires the replacement of deviant fantasies with appropriate fantasies while masturbating. With many offenders, impulsiveness and sexual arousal are the main issues, and they need both punishment and treatment.

According to Dr. Anderson (1990), "There are problems with extinguishing arousal patterns of the rapist because normal males respond to rape scenarios." This observation reflects prevalent male cultural attitudes about women. A study by Eugene Kanin on date rapists (Warshaw 1988) found that these men had adopted highly erotic-oriented peer group socialization that started during the junior-high years and continued through college. Sexual conquest became associated with their feelings of worth and thus were acceptable to them.

The statement by Dr. Anderson in the previous paragraph is another example of how males in our society have bought the myth that females really like rough sex. Many of the pornographic movies depict rape, and nonoffending males report arousal. After two decades of the newly sensitive nurturing male, the macho stud is back (Gelman et al. 1990). In sexually explicit movies and suggestive music videos, men flex their muscles and women surrender. This is a disheartening trend for our nation when ranked with other countries. The U.S. rape rate is four times that of Germany, thirteen times that of England, and twenty times that of Japan (U.S. House 1990). Perhaps men in the United States have mistaken sexual liberation for a license to assert themselves in an inappropriate way. They are given the cultural message that they must conquer to be manly.

Some helping professionals who assess rapists may choose to minimize the crime if they hold some of the same attitudes about women and sex. Some of them may have to admit to themselves that at some time in their lives, they forced a woman to have sex with them when she really didn't want to.

The lack of proper assessment and treatment of rapists can certainly be a second rape, not only for the survivor but also for society. How many rapists are out there waiting to ask your daughter for a date? How many looked so convincing in their psychological evaluations that no punishment was given or treatment mandated?

# PART FOUR

# Empowerment

# 12

# Survival Tactics
# for the Second Rape

## Preventive Attitudes

There is no assurance that a woman can totally protect herself against rape. Expressing herself in a more assertive manner may, however, lessen her risk. In an acquaintance or dating situation, women have a right to set sexual limits and communicate those limits. They need to establish the fact that any sexual activity will be mutual. In our culture, women have been taught that attractive femininity is passive and childlike. Women need to be more adult and assertive and still believe in themselves as desirable people when they behave in an assertive way.

Women have often given confusing messages to men regarding sex. When a woman says no, she must mean it. When she says yes, she needs to know what she is agreeing to. When a man ignores agreed upon sexual limits, a woman should act forcefully and decisively. A woman should yell or do whatever it takes to get others' attention, and she needs to forget about being polite.

Most women the authors interviewed had had some experiences in which sex was expected from them. One woman stated,

> I remember when I was sixteen years old and went to the drive-in movies with a boy I had met at my workplace. It was our first date, and I was a virgin. After a few kisses, he tried to fondle me and push for sex. I was enraged and felt violated. I told him that if he didn't stop I would yell rape, get out of the car, and go call my parents to pick me up. I got scared, but I was angry, too. How dare he expect

sex on a first date when we hardly knew each other? Luckily, he believed me and stopped insisting. He had the nerve to call me several times again for a date, but I refused. He didn't even apologize for what had happened. He just sort of acted cocky about it.

Another woman recalls an experience in college:

> I went on a fraternity outing with a guy, and the outing was called a woodsie. That's where you take alcohol and a blanket and go out into the woods and make out. He tried to persuade me to have sex and was shocked and a bit angry that I wouldn't. He made the comment that I was from a large city and he just assumed I had had a lot of sexual experiences. It was only when I threatened to yell rape so loud that others might hear that he backed off.

Women who act passively toward men may expect them to be dominant and forceful and fail to realize that an interaction is progressing toward rape (Warshaw 1988). Therefore, we need to educate our children at a young age that they have a right to behave assertively concerning their own bodies and sexuality. Girls need to be aware of steps that can lead to rape as well as dangerous situations to avoid. Boys need to learn respect for women regarding mutuality for sex. They also need to know that they can be charged with a criminal offense and served with a civil suit if they rape.

Education about assertiveness regarding protection of the body can begin in preschool. Several books have been written for young children about saying no to inappropriate touches and telling someone if that person persists (Gamble and Behana 1986). There are also programs using puppets for very young children on the same theme. Education about rape needs to continue in grade school, high school, and even college.

According to Robin Warshaw (1988), families and schools have avoided education concerning the issue of date rape. Parents of boys often feel that it is not their concern because they have boys. It is their concern, however, because boys are usually doing the raping. Parents of boys involved in acquaintance rape may be held liable in civil suits.

Educators also like to ignore the fact that rape exists on their own campuses. Most school officials do not want to risk calling attention to their campus rape because their reputation is at stake. In Mercedes's story, school officials were careful to keep publicity to a minimum to avoid parent hysteria regarding the possibility of rape on the campus. Schools can find themselves vulnerable to lawsuits if they admit to a lack of vigilence regarding rape.

One innovative and successful approach to educating men about rape is to have a male speaker or workshop leader impart that information. When male speakers talk to other men about this topic and admit that at one time or another their own sexual acts may not have been consensual, the men in the audience may listen more closely.

## Guidelines for Rape Survivors

1. Call a friend or loved one for immediate support. You need to choose whom you call carefully. It must be someone who is supportive and has a nonjudgmental attitude about rape.

2. Report the crime even if it is date rape. Reporting is empowering even though there are flaws in our system. Regardless of the outcome of reporting, rape is a serious charge, and we can expect that the attacker will feel humiliated and embarrassed because he has been charged with rape. There will likely be repercussions with his employer, parents, wife, or friends. Therefore, he will be punished no matter what the legal punishment is. In some rape cases, when the survivor knows her attacker, it may be advantageous to phone him and record the call, as he might say something incriminating in response to a direct confrontation.

3. Call a rape crisis center. It may have someone to help you navigate through the system from A to Z.

4. Do not shower, change clothes, urinate, or defecate, and go immediately to the emergency room of a hospital that does rape exams. You have nothing to lose by going to the hospital because you don't have to mention the offender's name.

5. If you want to have a familiar face in the emergency room, ask permission to call your own physician or gynecologist to meet you there. You should become acquainted with what his or her attitudes are concerning rape and with which hospital he or she is affiliated.

6. Have evidence collected even if you haven't decided whether to prosecute. You may decide to prosecute later, and a medical exam is a vital part of your case. Insist that you have an HIV test done for AIDS, paid for by the state, with an update every six months. Also insist that your attacker have the same test done, with an update every six months.

You can refuse to have the drug/alcohol screen. Some physicians choose to do this screen, and some do not. You are not the offender, and rape is the crime, not your alcohol or drug use.

7. Write down or tape-record your account of the rape as soon as possible. This cuts down on all contradictions written down by police, medical personnel, the district attorney, and others. A survivor is often in a state of shock when first interviewed, and missing or incorrect information can be inconsistent with information gathered later. Some written descriptions by professionals may be inaccurate because of inaccurate note taking.

Don't let shame stand in the way of telling the truth. A weapon is not necessary to substantiate a rape, and neither is force. After the initial shock wears off, you may remember more details of the crime. Call the police investigator or district attorney regarding these details.

8. Secure your home or stay with friends. Realize that the police will not be able to provide protection for you. If the offender knows your address and he is not apprehended, consider the possibility of moving.

9. Seek professional one-to-one counseling with an experienced person. Call a rape crisis hot line or a victim assistance program to find a qualified and screened therapist. The psychological work that needs to be done includes freeing yourself from the fears generated by the rape, acknowledging and bearing the pain caused by the rape, redefining your feelings of vulnerability and helplessness, and regaining control of your life (Burgess and Holmstrom 1979).

To proceed with life after the rape, it is necessary to access all of your feelings. A strong, experienced therapist will be able to share your discomfort so that you do not have to bear it alone.

A therapist can help you gain a sense of control by helping you to make numerous decisions: whether to move, get a new unlisted phone number, get job retraining, or take self-defense classes. You may be able to change lemons to lemonade by discovering a new part of yourself. You may find that you can help other rape victims. Often the experience of being raped can prompt survivors to go back to college for a degree in counseling. Because rape can happen to anyone, it is unusual that a survivor has severe psychopathology; therefore, healing can occur relatively quickly. You may eventually feel stronger than you did before the rape, and you may function with more tenacity.

Other members of the family often need therapy to understand your rape experience. Knowledge helps them to be more understanding and supportive of your feelings. Male partners especially need help in dealing with their own guilt about not protecting you. They need help with their anger toward the rapist and need to understand that blaming or condemning you is inappropriate and damaging.

Above all, you need to visualize yourself as a heroine. You are alive and have made it through a life-threatening situation; therefore, you deserve a medal.

10. Seek out group therapy for rape survivors. The commonality of a group experience will reassure you that you're not crazy and help you feel that you're not alone. A group experience also helps you depersonalize your maltreatment by helping professionals in the system as you learn that others are experiencing the same thing.

Women need to return to a communion of women. On a broader scale, the group could consist of daughters, mothers, or girlfriends who support you as you go to court. The group could become politically active and push for tougher sentencing for rapists or further victim's rights legislation.

11. If your phone calls to the police or district attorney are not returned, be persistent. The system is overloaded, with the number of cases often exceeding the number of personnel to handle them. You must be assertive here, as often the squeaky wheel gets the grease. Be careful, however, not to alienate those working on your behalf by attacking their competency. Ask your counselor for help on assertive communication skills.

12. Request a new district attorney if you determine that yours is unsympathetic or has personal bias against rape victims. You can do this by asking to speak to the supervisor of district attorneys.

13. Talk to your district attorney about questions that may arise from the defense concerning your sexual life and how you should handle those questions.

14. Insist that you have some input and are informed regarding the plea-bargaining process.

15. Ask who is doing the psychological evaluation of the offender and see if he or she will give you some time to tell your version of what happened or any facts that may be pertinent to the assessment of the offender's dangerousness.

16. Know that you have a right to speak at the sentencing of your attacker. Let the judge know specifics about how the attack has changed or inhibited your life-style and functioning. Let him or her know what you think is fair punishment for the crime.

17. Don't put your life on hold for the trial. This gives your attacker more power than he deserves. The night before the scheduled trial, review the notes that you have taken throughout the process so that you can feel confident that you are accurate in your testimony.

18. Have plenty of outlets for your frustration and anger. Become physically active to help alleviate stress. Have a variety of support people to whom you can turn. If none of them is available, vent your feelings by writing.

19. Read books on rape to educate yourself on the crime and its effects on you and others, and encourage those close to you to read them, too.

20. Speak with the offender's parole officer after sentencing so that you can be informed of his location and when he will be released from custody.

21. Explore the possibility of some form of victim compensation in your state. You may be entitled to reimbursement for lost wages, medical expenses, damaged property, and travel expenses to and from the courthouse. You may need to have some time off from your job and may qualify for disability payments from your employer.

## Other Alternatives

If you do not wish to press criminal charges and you were raped on a college campus, you can bring the case before the university judicial board. The judgments on these cases, which are usually date rapes, appear to be mild (Warshaw 1988). The offender may be asked to write an essay on rape or be suspended briefly. Some university officials feel that being brought before the board has an effect on the accused by drawing attention to his crime.

Civil suits are another means of survivor empowerment. In criminal court, the burden of proof is on the prosecution to convince twelve jurors that the defendant committed the rape beyond a reasonable doubt. In civil courts, however, the standard changes to only a preponderance of evidence to substantiate guilt. Obviously, this is much easier to prove and can result in far greater feelings of empowerment for the survivor.

A personal injury attorney can file suit on behalf of a survivor. The purpose of this action is not the imprisonment or punishment of the rapist, which is in the hands of the state. A personal injury suit results in some type of compensation, most often for the survivor's injuries resulting from the crime. These legal actions are in the hands of the survivor and the attorney she has hired to represent her.

As with criminal cases, there is a statute of limitations for filing personal injury suits. This is important because the survivor can get so bogged down in the criminal process that she misses the filing date. A common misconception is that the defendant must be found guilty in criminal court before a civil suit is filed. A personal injury attorney clarified this point:

> We do the same thing that the district attorney does, but it's easier to prove. We still need to collect evidence, and we should get it when it's fresh. In general, however, women who are raped fare better in civil suits. It's not an all or nothing proposition like in criminal court. If we do our homework and make progress in the discovery process, chances are the case won't go to trial and will be settled out of court.

If the survivor's assaulter has money, it is possible to sue him directly for damages. In many cases, however, the assaulter has no money, and a third party who is shown to be negligent for the commission of the crime is sued. Most often this third party is insured. An important distinction between *negligence* and *intentional acts* must be made. Negligence is human error committed without the purpose of doing harm. Intentional acts are done with the explicit motivation of committing a wrong and doing harm. Insurance companies exclude intentional acts from coverage. Using auto damages as an example, if a person takes his car and uses it as a weapon to hit another car, this act would be excluded from insurance compensation. If, however, the person looked left when he should have looked right and caused a collision, this would be covered. Likewise, if the man of the house raped the woman, she would not be entitled to compensation on his home owner's liability policy.

There are many possible sources of negligence. As one attorney said, the trick is to be imaginative. This attorney stated,

> If an apartment complex holds itself out as being secure, you should expect that there are minimum safety precautions for the residents. For instance, if there is an electronically operated gate, it should actually work. If a building is in a high crime area, it may be negligent not to have a security guard to patrol the grounds. It is implied that reasonable care is to be taken to make sure buildings are safe. Not to do so may constitute negligence.

As further examples, one of the authors counseled a woman who sued a large hotel for having unsafe lighting in its parking lot, where she was accosted, kidnapped, and later gang-raped. In another case, this author counseled a child after an attempted rape by a next-door neighbor teen. The crime occurred in the neighbor's bathroom. The teen's mother was shown to be negligent because she had knowledge of her son's propensity to act in a harmful way with younger children. Sometime previously, the teen had walked in on another neighbor girl while she was in the bathroom and had attempted to do the same thing. The mother knew of this previous event and failed to exercise necessary care in the prevention of a second attempted rape. The mother's home owner's policy covered her negligence, and the child received half a million dollars in damages.

One of the biggest questions asked by survivors is how much money they can expect from a civil suit. One personal injury attorney noted,

> In terms of compensation, the biggest factor is the residual problems resulting from a rape. A broken nose can heal, but the mind doesn't heal. We draw a life sketch of the survivor before and after the rape. The more a woman's life has changed for the worse, the higher the

amount of damages. Mostly we are talking about psychological damages such as continued distrust of men. A woman who's been raped is also entitled to be compensated for lost wages or, as is often the case, lost jobs.

One change in society that some personal injury attorneys noted is the greater recognition of psychological injuries resulting from trauma. One said, "Mental health professionals are no longer thought of as witch doctors. Sometimes a client will come in to see me saying they want to talk to a psychologist about their problems. If I suggest therapy, it is better received by my client."

It would be advisable for anybody who has survived a rape and suffered loss and pain—emotional or physical—to have her particular circumstances analyzed by professional legal counsel. In most cases, there is no charge for a consultation, and if the attorney decides to represent the survivor, no retainer is needed up front. Customarily, attorneys take part of the settlement—one-quarter in the case of minors and one-third with adults. The scope of this book does not allow for a detailed analysis of personal injury law, but investigating this form of legal action within the first year after rape often leads to a survivor's greater empowerment.

We hope that the tactics described here will help educate and empower rape survivors. The survivor needs to assert herself at a time when she may feel the most vulnerable in her life. This is not an easy task, but it will pay off in the long run by increasing her self-esteem and feelings of control. These tactics will not take away her pain but will help her take an active role in coping with the second rape.

# 13

## Toward a New View of
## Men and Women

**C**learly, our justice system may not tell us what really happened in a rape or who was at fault. The filing of a police report, the decision to prosecute, the plea bargain, and the trial are issues of judgment rather than truth. These judgments—whether made by a male or a female—reflect a patriarchal foundation of reasoning and beliefs about gender roles in our present-day society. The judgments are not necessarily moral and certainly not absolute. An alternative way of defining rape and men and women does exist—in fact it has existed for about thirty thousand years.

It is the misfortune of a woman raped now (or perhaps in the last two thousand years) that the prevalent view of how things are favors rigid sex-role stereotypes—that is, definitions of masculinity synonymous with violent aggression and domination and definitions of femininity synonymous with masochism and shame. It is important always to remember that society can be wrong in its current point of view. The good news is that since men and women once lived within humanistic and egalitarian structures, they can return. We are not suggesting something new or impossible but an approach that is fundamental to our species. Getting there, however, requires both evolutionary and revolutionary change on a massive level. This change is the only way to prevent the first rape and the second rape.

In terms of recovery, women need to depersonalize the experience of rape. The way a survivor is treated when she decides to seek justice has nothing to do with her as a person—whether she wore a short skirt, drank alcohol, or went immediately to the emergency room. It has everything to do with whether she was lucky enough to be assigned a police officer, mental or medical personnel, legal counsel, judge, and jury who were aware of what rape is really about.

Men and women everywhere need to view rape as a political issue. For the most part, the experience of seeking justice is a form of political punishment designed to keep women in their place, ashamed of their sexuality and afraid to be themselves. The second rape is still a witch-hunt. In fact, if it works, it deters women from reporting a rape or following through on a report. Thus far, this tactic has been very successful.

To politicize rape rather than to personalize it requires knowledge about alternative ways in which men and women can be defined and can interact to give each other greater power and choices. In the past three decades, more and more has been written about definitions of masculinity and femininity. In this chapter, we hope to convey some of this knowledge. To learn, it is necessary to read with an openness and willingness to depart from accepted thinking. As Wilhelm Reich once said, at this point in history, changing the objective socioeconomic systems is not enough. Repressive behavior; sadistic power relations; competition to exploit, dominate, and humiliate; and our accommodations to these insults are by now conditioned into the nervous system of each member of our "civilized" societies. Both oppressors and victims are damaged by the experience. We are "wired for oppression" (Sjöö and Mor 1987, 18). The next section offers suggestions for rewiring our thoughts on masculinity.

## Masculinity

The goal in human revolution and evolution is not merely to change the guard by having women dominate male behavior. Men have been oppressed as long as women. As with women, the oppressive wiring of the nervous system occurs at the most intimate levels of existence—sexual and spiritual.

Nearly all people value human actions according to the gender of the one who acts—that is, some things are wrong for a woman to do but right for a man and vice versa. Especially in the sexual arena, we blindly and with steadfast faith accept certain values about behavior as if they were biological facts. In reality, we have no idea why or how these ideas came to be accepted as truisms. For a man in a sexual encounter, the foremost concern is whether he will be acting like a man—or *not* acting like a woman. A man's gender identity is defined, in part, by whether he is forceful and dominant, perhaps even aggressive, in relation to women. This is considered the way men are. It is a rationale upheld by society with no basis in fact.

As if these constraints were not enough, a man must adopt an illogical perspective with regard to sex. As John Stoltenberg (1989) writes, one way in which men are oppressed is by forcing members of this gender to adopt rapist ethics if they are to be viewed as masculine by society. These rapist ethics affirm a structural view of personal responsibility for acts as right or wrong but portray the one to whom the act is done as being responsible for the act (like the driver of a car believing that the tree beside the road caused the collision). Furthermore, this reversal of moral accountability (a dramatic projection) is characteristic of nearly all acts committed within the ethic of male sexual identity. "She made me do it" is the litany of the real man, followed by a response from society that reinforces his obliviousness to consequence, egotism, and willfulness. Forgiveness, Stoltenberg adds, is elicited by men at critical moments, only to seduce the woman back into victimization.

Perhaps the greatest delusion is that there is such a thing as a "real man." The male sex is socially constructed. It is a political entity that would cease to exist were it not for acts of force and sexual terrorism. A man must do some act to a woman to make her feel inferior and less powerful so that he may realize his membership in the masculinity club. Treating another human being as less worthy of respect would seem to be an act that would morally trouble some men, and probably it does.

There are individuals with penises and individuals with vaginas. Masculinity as a cluster of role or gender-typed behaviors is a lie. Individuals with both sex organs are capable of a wide range of varied behaviors. Not to be free to express all aspects of your self is oppression in its purest form. But the lie forces men to engage in rapelike behaviors that will make the male sex seem real. According to Stoltenberg (1989),

> We all grow up knowing exactly what kind of sex that is. It's the kind of sex you can have when you pressure or bully someone else into it. So it's a kind of sex that makes your will more important than theirs. That kind of sex helps the lie a lot. That kind of sex makes you feel like someone important and it turns the other person into someone unimportant. That kind of sex makes you feel real, not like a fake. It's the kind of sex men have in order to feel like a real man.
>
> There's also the kind of sex you can have when you force someone and hurt someone and cause someone suffering and humiliation. Violence and hostility in sex help the lie a lot too. Real men are aggressive in sex. Real men get cruel in sex. Real men use their penises like weapons in sex. Real men leave bruises. Real men think it's a turn-on to threaten harm. . . . It's the kind of sex men have in order to have a manhood. (p. 35)

Men also write that there is a fairly common compulsion among their gender to feel as though they should have sex even when they don't feel like it. Unless they are experiencing their bodies in a way that is explicitly, culturally, and sexually phallic, men don't feel their identity. Of course, the pornography industry is only too glad to assist men in their arousal—not so they can have fulfilling intimate lives but so they can feel their masculine identity. That is oppression. They also relearn to objectify female bodies in the process, which alienates them further.

Masculinity needs to be rethought. Although new role models have not replaced old ones, they have grown alongside them. A dynamic tension exists now between the macho seducer and loving companion—between Rambo and Phil Donahue (Kimmel 1987). Some men are exploring new options in life-style. Spurred on by the women's movement, they are learning that they have missed a lot by not sharing in the household and spending more time with their children. And men have suffered physically and emotionally by living up to the standards of masculinity. This standard can only be isolating and restrictive in its emphasis on always being strong. Men are gradually learning to express a wider range of feelings more deeply to women and other men. At the same time, violence against women and homophobia seem to be increasing. It is the hope of researchers on masculinity that the tension of opposition might bring about a new synthesis and relief from the oppression of membership in this gender class.

Women's studies are taught in most U.S. universities, and a trend toward men's studies as a separate course has become visible. The latter seeks to treat masculinity not as being normative referent but as a gender construct that has problems and is open to social scientific study.

Recent men's studies by Donnerstein and Linz (1987) revealed that although the combination of sexual explicitness and violence against women (pornographic conditions) resulted in the highest levels of subsequent aggression against a female target, the nonexplicit depiction that showed only violence resulted in aggression levels nearly as high and attitudes that were more callous than those that resulted from the combined condition. These are the pervasive messages in our media in general, from prime-time television to popular films. In a real sense, our society teaches and fosters aggressiveness against women. Our society teaches men callous attitudes about rape. Even if a woman seems repelled by a pursuer, eventually she will respond favorably to forceful advances. In other words, sexual aggression is profitable. The negative impact that derives from long-term exposure to women in scenes of degradation and subordination cannot be underestimated.

Other studies such as those by Thompson and Pleck (1987) identify core imperatives of the male role as seeking achievement, cultivating independence and self-confidence, developing a penchant for aggressiveness, and suppressing emotion. The most salient prescriptive, however, is that a male not do or feel anything feminine. As a group, four hundred men in a research sample of collegiate men indicated that they did not fully endorse these traditional male norms. That this normative orientation is weak in younger, educated men suggests that gender roles are not fixed and static and that masculinity is, in fact, a social construct. Most of all, it lends optimism for a real change and a decrease in the incidence of rape.

There is also the hope that a credo can be adopted by men about behavior in sexual relationships that will reverse the damage of centuries—damage that casts them in the role of the oppressor so that they feel okay about who they are. According to John Stoltenberg (1989), not living the big lie means several specific things:

1. Freely given informed consent from your partner is absolutely necessary. If a woman is disabled, intoxicated, or asleep, she cannot give informed consent. If a male is unsure about consent, he should ask her specifically. If there is still doubt, he should ask her again, remembering that consent for one act is not consent for another. Nothing can be taken for granted—even if the man meets the woman in a bar or she is wearing a miniskirt.

2. A feeling of mutuality for your partner is absolutely necessary. This means that a man does not relate sexually to a woman as an object or as someone he does something to. Sex is something you do *with* another and feel *with* another. It is an experience of whole bodies. It means paying attention to your partner—her verbal and nonverbal messages—as if they were as important as your own.

3. Respect for your partner is absolutely essential. This means that your partner has the right to withdraw, say no, and go home at any time and that her body always has integrity. She is not your possession, whether it is the first time or the hundredth time you've had relations. A man does not have the right to disrespect a woman's feelings or body through physical or verbal intimidation.

4. Men can choose not to be manipulated by a culture that sells the objectifying and conquering of women. This could mean refusing to buy pornography, to view certain television shows or movies, or to listen to certain music that objectifies women.

5. Men can choose not to have their sex lives numbed or tricked by alcohol, drugs, or any substance that interferes with the ability to make clear choices or send clear messages.

6. Men can choose how and when they want to have a sexual relationship without the demands of proving anything to their partner or the guys in the locker room. Gender role expectations have no business in an intimate encounter. If sex is work or something a man has to do, he is living the lie.

Dualistic thinking, with its categories of discrete gender categories and hierarchies of power, has done its harm. When men must compete with each other to be "real men," fearing feminine behavior in each other and themselves, they become estranged from their own gender. When men exclude women, they become estranged from part of themselves. As Sjöö and Mor (1987) write, "There is no freedom for males of any class or color or ethnic group, while the female remains unfree" (p. 70).

## Femininity

If, according to gender role stereotypes, men are socially conditioned to be rapists, women are socially conditioned to be victims. Sigmund Freud said that submission and suffering were the due of all women and, furthermore, that they enjoyed it. Elements in our culture today continually reinforce this assessment. At this stage in history, a large majority of women *do* need to be trained to stand up for themselves. Assertion does not come naturally for women because it causes anxiety. Women *are* more prone to feelings of guilt and hyperresponsibility. Women *do* have a long way to go in overcoming masochism, the defense mechanism responsible for so many of women's problems with assaultive crimes and the legal system.

The term *masochism* in its most general use denotes the derivation of pleasure from painful circumstances. As a defense mechanism used by many women, it seeks to prevent or extinguish hostile aggression in others. According to Natalie Shainess (1984), overuse makes women prone to a personality warp wherein they tend to apologize too often, are hypersuggestible, accept the premise of the other, avoid questioning, capitulate to the other's view, and equivocate for fear of taking responsibility for their own decisions. Like Little Red Riding Hood, they may say more than is necessary and put themselves in jeopardy. They may fail to heed their own internal cues of danger and misinterpret ambiguous situations. Clearly, nice girls don't fight. The corollary is that they are too busy fending off others to take care of themselves.

Acquiescence and accommodation are translated into victim-prone nonverbal behaviors. For the rapist, a woman who slouches, avoids eye contact, and carries herself with little assurance is a good target. When he unexpectedly confronts her and threatens harm, she cries and remains passive to fend him off. Like a deer in a gesture of capitulation, she bares her throat to her opponent, and he goes for the jugular.

In the courtroom as a witness, a masochistic woman will have problems maintaining and projecting a clear and accurate perspective. The jury may view the woman's metamessages of femininity with contempt rather than pity. Her crying, her head nodding, her avoidance of eye contact, and her indecisiveness may be mistaken for guilt and shame. The process of pressing charges is difficult because it is often ambiguous. Visual cues and tone of voice can be overly personalized by a masochistic woman—sometimes incorrectly. The legal process is gray until the end, but the masochistic woman thinks in terms of black and white—for instance, "If my district attorney doesn't return my phone call, it must be because he doesn't believe me." In her quest for absolute protection from the risk of harm, she may arrive at the wrong conclusion. Masochistic thinking designed to fend off the anxiety of possible harm leads to behavior that can alienate others and damage the case. It certainly brings the pain she expected for those acts of femininity she's been conditioned to believe are pleasurable.

There may be other reasons why women fare so poorly emotionally in our legal system. Early socialization experiences and the rigid gender typecasting they are assigned make it difficult for women to tolerate the level of conflict inherent in a legal situation. According to Jean Baker Miller (1986), it is against the grain of a woman's development for her to value herself more highly than her affiliations. Women have been conditioned to value relationships with others most of all.

Based on studies of the differences between male and female development, little girls do not like rules. If a dispute arises in a game, they'll either disregard the rules or end the game so that everyone can remain friends. Little boys, however, enjoy the dispute. They'll keep fighting it out. The rules are preserved, but relationships are easily replaced (Gilligan 1982). A woman adhering to her gender type of femininity may find it distinctly negative to follow the rules of law, which may cause the suspect (who may be a spouse, former lover, or coworker) to hate her. A woman's first instinct would be to overlook a wrong and not make waves—in fact, not to report a crime if a relationship is at stake.

According to the research reported by Carol Gilligan (1982), not only do females view aggression as a fracture of a connection and a sign of failure, but they have developed an uncertainty about their right to make moral statements. George Eliot speaks of a female's "susceptibleness" to adverse judgments from others, stemming from her lack of power and consequent inability "to do something in the world" (Gilligan 1982, 66). Since women may believe themselves to have no choice in society, they excuse themselves from the responsibility of making decisions that could work in their behalf.

Femininity does not teach aggressiveness as a valuable behavior, nor does it validate a woman's ability to judge. Both components are needed to be a successful survivor. As it is now, a rape survivor may debate her own version of moral justice and focus on how others will view her situation and whether they will agree with her sometimes tentative conclusion.

Masculinity tells a man to have a skewed sense of responsibility. It tells him he can externalize the blame for his actions onto women and at the same time take responsibility for her choices. Femininity teaches a woman a reverse sense of responsibility, which is just as illogical. It tells her to take the responsibility for the actions of others while allowing others to be responsible for her choices. Both are backward in their assumptions.

Self-assertion exposes a woman to criticism. The legal system exposes a woman to criticism. Both are hard terrain for femininity, which teaches her that she will lose her sensitivity and compassion once she acquires the power of her own knowledge and exercises her rights and responsibilities as an adult. Like masculinity, femininity is a myth. It tells women they need to be taken care of to be okay.

Women have lost their natural powers and wisdom, the legacy of ancient ages. Women grow up today learning to disregard the effects of their own bodily rhythms, cycles, needs, and capacities. Years and years of being told their bodies are evil and subversive have left them with a pervasive sense of shame and humiliation about natural functions. Women now have a cultural heritage of being punished as autonomous and sexual beings. It is little wonder that women who meet the unwanted sexual advances of men feel ashamed and unclean as a first response. It is little wonder that women who are raped start to think of themselves as the evil seductress who caused it to happen. Self-blame and confusion, the legacy of patriarchy, come easy.

Female collectives once built and created. They cooperated and nurtured each other for the advancement of humankind. Women's rituals and ceremonies united humans. Music, dancing, and utterances had a binding significance that released life forces into harmonious activity. Female techniques were not manipulated for personal profit or exploited for personal power.

Now women function as their own worst enemies, fighting each other as they are, on patriarchal terrain. Patriarchy thrives on human discord. It is essential that humankind be broken up into economic enemies, racial enemies, political enemies, religious enemies, worker against worker, white against dark, man against woman, man against man, woman against woman (Sjöö and Mor 1987). Women have lost trust in themselves. But perhaps the saddest truth is that they have lost trust in each other.

In Greek myths, patriarchy played with the goddess, who was both strong and compassionate. She was broken into fragments, and the fragments were pitted against each other in jealous bickering. As Sjöö and Mor (1987) state, "Women were isolated and collectives broken up by forcibly capturing and imprisoning female energy within the patriarchal family" (p. 241). From then on, women passed from the guardianship of their father to their husband and finally to their oldest son. Women become estranged from their cosmic unity and spiritual identity. They were demoralized and have never recovered.

The modern working woman exercising her newfound rights becomes (or tries to become) a male warrior adopting the values of patriarchy to compensate for the feelings of powerlessness that come with her gender. She enters the battlefield of the workplace and becomes part of what Tara Roth Madden (1987) calls "urban guerrilla warfare" (p. 1). The uncivil civil war she speaks of, however, is not between male and female but between females: between women of different socioeconomic classes and different generations, with their contrasting values, ambitions, and expectations. Those vying to move up from the working and lower classes are pitted against middle-class women, who are trying to prevent a backslide. Very few women make it to the top of corporate America.

According to Madden, fighting among women in the workplace is driven by the fear that they will fail socially and economically.

But it is fostered by an ongoing rivalry that women learn beginning when they are children. Females compete with each other for who will be seen as more acceptable in the eyes of the world. Before entering the workplace, the rivalry was confined to who was the prettiest and who got the best mate. This competition has carried over into the workplace and manifests itself as lying, backstabbing, character assassination, and the sabotage of other women who pose a threat to their work position. As a result, women become more concerned with holding each other back than with just going forward. Meanwhile, men forge ahead to the top and watch the scratching and hissing with amusement.

Women have learned well to hide their real feelings. At the root of the rivalry between different factions of women often lies a fear of masculine attitudes in ambitious women—particularly young career-oriented women. Their "bragging" and "aggressiveness" is attacked by women who still extol the virtues of home and husband while viewing a job as a temporary or economically necessary diversion from their real worth.

To say that women are not united is an understatement. The woman who wants to feel power in a patriarchal sense goes it alone. Women do not help each other. They don't support each other's self-image. They lay roadblocks in front of each other, and these are compounded by the patriarchal business of Madison Avenue, which makes women feel as if they never look good enough and that this is the sum total of their self-worth (Madden 1987).

There is another side to this coin that has negative ramifications for the survivor of rape. She cannot count on her own gender to support her. In their climb to the top of patriarchal institutions, many women have lost the compassion of sisterhood. It would seem that some women who have finally found top places in society forsake femininity as vulnerable and dangerous. Our interviews with female prosecutors and female police detectives demonstrated what on the surface appeared to be cool detachment but reeked of contempt for women who let their femininity show. "I'm not like them; it could never happen to me" was a common remark made by women in survivor-helping professions. Men have been acculturated to be the rescuers and safekeepers of femininity. As one woman said, "They're better at playing the sympathy game." Survivors who turn in need to other women may meet with suspicion and disregard rather than caring and understanding. Women who have conformed to the values of patriarchal institutions hate their other half. To own this half is to admit that *all* women have a problem and must do something.

In doing something, women should return to their forgotten heritage for answers. Women can learn from the credo adopted by the goddess cultures of long ago. From what we know, these women were not rape victims. The big lie of femininity, like the big lie of masculinity, rests on people being only half of themselves. To correct this problem, women must take several specific steps:

1. *Women must reown their bodies.* This means no more dissociation. Women should be well acquainted with the internal processes of their bodies and heed their messages. They should place their bodies in high regard and take the responsibility of ownership for their protection and treatment by others.

2. *Women must reown their sexuality.* This means adopting clearer sexual moral values. The independent goddess never engaged in sexual relations to keep a man, please a man at her own expense, or be accepted by her peers. For instance, casual sex and pleasure separated from love were adamantly opposed by the love goddess Aphrodite (Harrow 1990). The goal of sex for the ancients was the union of love and pleasure, the transcendence of body and spirit, and the sacred act of bringing beautiful moments of mutual sharing and creativity to a loved one. It was never something they endured or passively allowed to happen. Sex carries with it heavy responsibilities for conscious decisions and clear messages about sexual values and limits.

3. *Women must reown their intuition.* This especially refers to paying attention to gut-level feelings of discomfort and danger within relationships. Women should trust their inner selves even if that means "creating a scene," causing disapproval, or not being polite. Women need to assert their intuition by sending clear messages.

4. *Women must reown their anger and aggression.* This means not being afraid to become aggressive or take charge of a situation if it's called for. This is especially so if assertion (saying stop or no)

fails. The ancient goddess was both strong and compassionate. Women must stop believing that suffering and pain are attractive features. They can end most of their suffering by learning skills of assertion and self-defense.

5. *Women can choose not to be manipulated* by a culture that sells the objectifying and exploitation of their gender, whether this is depicted in popular magazines, books, television shows, videos, or movies.

6. *Women can choose not to have their romantic lives numbed or tricked* by alcohol, drugs, or any substance that interferes with their ability to make clear choices and send clear messages.

7. *Women can choose partners and dates who treat them as equals* and with mutual respect.

With all this said, the question that begs to be asked is "Why should women adopt patriarchal values?" There is, after all, a good argument for men adopting matrifocal values. Some would say that with patriarchy, we have created a world of rampant violence that is increasing as we "progress." Some would say that we have become alienated machines with a quality of life resembling the desperate quest of a rat's maze. As Sjöö and Mor (1987) state,

> The average adult member of a hunting-and-gathering culture—even in some environments called sparse by our standards—worked only fifteen hours a week to fill sustenance needs. The rest of the time was spent in leisure activity: arts and crafts, spiritual ecstasy, running, swimming, making love, laughing, eating, goofing around. (p. 43)

How ironic that with "progress" the average man's workweek is forty-five hours and the average woman's is seventy-seven hours. Leisure time in the United States is decreasing. Some would call this cultural regression.

Women need to return to traditional female values of trust, caring, intimacy, affiliation, and maintenance, and these must be given their just place in civilization. In a world too full of violence and oppression, we don't need more masculine values of aggression, power, and control. We are beckoned to return to a cooperative/communal system that allows us all to work side by side as equals with a common goal of peace. Training and education need to be undertaken in the home, school, and community so that all people can learn to use and value all aspects of themselves. Both men and women have creative female energy, and it is this energy that has the power to heal and bond and to save us from destruction.

We hope that humankind is entering an era of concern about humanitarianism. We need to look not only at our foolhardy and selfish exploitation of our planet but also at its inhabitants. We need to stop raping mother earth and the mother goddess once and for all.

# References

Anderson, Ray. 1990. Personal communication, October 16.

Bart, Pauline, and Patricia O'Brien. 1986. *Stopping Rape: Successful Survival Strategies.* Aberdeen, Scotland: Pergamon Press.

Bettleheim, Bruno. 1976. *The Uses of Enchantment: The Meaning and Importance of Fairy Tales.* New York: Random House.

Brownmiller, Susan. 1975. *Against Our Will: Men, Women and Rape.* New York: Simon and Schuster.

Burgess, Ann Wolbert, and Lynda Lytle Holmstrom. 1979. *Rape Crisis and Recovery.* Bowie, Maryland: Robert J. Brady Co.

Cohen, Murray, Nicholas Groth, and Richard Siegel. 1978. "The Clinical Prediction of Dangerousness." *Crime and Delinquency, 24,* no. 1 (January), 28–39.

Donnerstein, Edward, and Daniel Linz. 1987. "Mass-Media Sexual Violence and Male Viewers: Current Theory and Research." In *Changing Men: New Directions in Research on Men and Masculinity,* edited by Michael S. Kimmel, p. 198–215. Newbury Park, California: Sage Publications.

Eisler, Riane. 1987. *The Chalice and the Blade: Our History, Our Future.* San Francisco: Harper and Row.

Estrich, Susan. 1987. *Real Rape.* Cambridge, Massachusetts: Harvard University Press.

Finkelhor, David, and Kersti Yllo. 1985. *License to Rape: Sexual Abuse of Wives.* New York: Free Press.

Gamble, Nancy, and Nory Behana. 1986. *No! Go! Tell!* San Diego: Grossmont College Press.

Gelman, David, Karen Springen, Regina Elam, Nadine Joseph, Kate Robins, and Mary Hager. 1990. "Mind of the Rapist." *Newsweek,* July 23, 46–52.

Gilligan, Carol. 1982. *In a Different Voice: Psychological Theory and Women's Development.* Cambridge, Massachusetts: Harvard University Press.

Grant, Toni. 1988. *Being a Woman: Fulfilling Your Femininity and Finding Love.* New York: Random House.

Groth, Nicholas. 1979. *Men Who Rape*. New York: Plenum Press.

Harrow, Judy. 1990. "A Season with Aphrodite." *Gnosis Magazine*, Fall 1990, 16–19.

Kimmel, Michael S. 1987. "Rethinking Masculinity." In *Changing Men: New Directions in Research on Men and Masculinity*, edited by Michael S. Kimmel, p. 9–24. Newbury Park, California: Sage Publications.

Madden, Tara Roth. 1987. *Women vs. Women: The Uncivil Business War*. New York: AMACOM, a division of American Management Association.
Meloy, Reid. 1989. Personal communication, September 7.
Miller, Jean Baker. 1986. *Toward a New Psychology of Women*. 2d ed. Boston: Beacon Press.

Saholz, Eloise, Karen Springen, Nonny de la Pena, and Debbie Witherspoon. 1990. "The Frightening Aftermath: Concern About AIDS Adds to the Trauma of Rape." *Newsweek*, July 23, 53.
Shainess, Natalie. 1984. *Sweet Suffering: Woman as Victim*. Indianapolis: Bobbs-Merrill.
Sjöö, Monica, and Barbara Mor. 1987. *The Great Cosmic Mother: Rediscovering the Religion of the Earth*. San Francisco: Harper and Row.
Stoltenberg, John. 1989. *Refusing to Be a Man: Essays on Sex and Justice*. Portland, Oregon: Breitenbush Books.

Thompson, Edward H., Jr., and Joseph H. Pleck. 1987. "The Structure of Male Role Norms." In *Changing Men: New Directions in Research on Men and Masculinity*, edited by Michael S. Kimmel, p. 25–36. Newbury Park, California: Sage Publications.

U.S. Congress. House. Select Committee on Children, Youth and Families. 1990. *Hearing on Victims of Rape*, June 28.

Walker, Lenore E. 1979. *The Battered Woman*. New York: Harper and Row.
Warshaw, Robin. 1988. *I Never Called It Rape*. New York: Harper and Row.

# Index

# Index

# About the
# Authors

Lee Madigan, Ph.D., and Nancy Gamble, Ph.D., are psychologists with private practices in Southern California. They specialize in treating rape survivors, women who were molested as children, and children identified as victims of violent crimes. Dr. Gamble is coauthor of the preschool book *No! Go! and Tell!* Dr. Madigan is on the board of directors of a Southern California rape crisis network.